COOK IN ISRAEL
HOME COOKING INSPIRATION

With Orly Ziv

Photographs by **Katherine Martinelli**

ISBN 978-965-92071-0-7

Text copyright ©2013 by Orly Ziv

Photographs copyright ©2013 by Katherine Martinelli

Designed by Idit Yatzkan

First Edition
Fourth Print
Orly Ziv
wwww.cookinisrael.com

■

I dedicate this book with lots of love to
*my soul mate and partner **Ben-Zvi***
*and my children **Dan**, **Dorine** and **Daniella**.*

I also dedicate this book
in the memory of my beloved parents
***Malka** & **David** who instilled in me*

the love for food.

■

Foreword

I first met Orly two years ago when I attended one of her tours of Tel Aviv's Carmel Market and a follow-up cooking class in her home. I was writing an article on culinary tours in Israel and she instantly captivated me with her warmth, knowledge, and simple, healthy approach to food. For a food writer who had recently moved to Israel, it was the ultimate introduction to Israeli home cooking.

Orly's recipes quickly worked their way into my repertoire. After just one class, her cauliflower with tahini and silan (p. 84) became my go-to side dish for entertaining, and I couldn't believe the picture perfect challah (p. 132) that I was able to recreate at home.

So when Orly approached me about working on a cookbook together, I didn't have to give it a second thought. I knew that I wouldn't just be photographing and editing the recipes - I'd have

a front row seat at the best cooking class in town. And after watching Orly prepare every single one of these dishes (and, more importantly, tasting them!) I can honestly say that I'm a better cook.

But you don't have to travel to Tel Aviv to get these lessons. Orly has chosen her best and most cherished recipes and presented them in this cookbook in a way so clear, so simple, that even the novice home chef can follow along. She was adamant about including a photo for every dish, and step-by-step photos for many of the recipes, so readers can know exactly what to expect in a finished product. She has also included helpful tips throughout - true nuggets of wisdom to make cooking easier and food taste better.

Week after week I traveled to Orly's home in Ramat Hasharon, just north of Tel Aviv, to work on this cookbook. We set up my minimal photography equipment in her dining room and kitchen, working around her family as they came and went. I felt a part of the Ziv household by the end of it, and I believe this cookbook offers that same personal insight. The book was a labor of love, a fact that shines through so clear and strong I believe you won't be able to help but feel it.

Cook in Israel: Home Cooking Inspiration captures the multifaceted, international spirit of Israeli cuisine by drawing on culinary inspiration from throughout the region and the globe. Orly pulls from her Jewish-Greek heritage, as well as recipes and techniques she's learned from friends, neighbors, television programs and cookbooks over the years. You'll find Moroccan, Egyptian, Bukharan, Turkish and Arab recipes alongside her son's favorite onion tart and her daughter's beloved chocolate cake. These are the recipes her family knows and loves, ones Orly makes again and again - and you will too.

Katherine Martinelli
Food Writer and Photographer

Introduction

I come by my love of food naturally. My mother, a talented Sephardic cook from Greece, was a recipe collector and food lover who encouraged my presence - and independence - in the kitchen. I started baking when I was 10 years old and before long was making all the desserts for the family. I also began a recipe collection of my own and would scribble notes all over them so I could remember what I did differently and if I would make it again.

When I was deciding what to study, my mother suggested nutrition as I had a passion for food and enjoyed reading about the healthy side of it. I became a clinical dietitian and worked for many years in the field, but part of me always wanted to be involved in tourism. Finally, years later, I was able to combine the two by offering culinary tours and cooking classes to travelers in Israel. I started Cook in Israel in 2009 and my vision has been to introduce Israel through home cooking and food culture.

My tours and classes - like the recipes in this book - reflect my personal tastes and interest in healthy, clean eating. I always take visitors to the shuk, the lively outdoor market that is the culinary heart and pulse of any Israeli city. Then we return to my home, where we cook a meal inspired by the market and fresh flavors of Israel alongside my family. For me food is an awakening of all the senses and cooking and baking is pure creativity.

This book is all thanks to my three children, who for years have been telling me to write it. With their encouragement, I was inspired to put pen to paper and leave my family with a memory of the flavors of home. I know how much I miss not having my mother and grandmother's recipes written down and wanted to give my kids something tangible to hold onto.

I've been vegetarian for almost 30 years and so you'll find little meat in these pages. My family loves meatballs and hashwa (rice with meat), so I make them on occasion and have included those recipes here. I've never liked chicken and don't cook it, so there's not a single chicken recipe to be found. I do, however, eat fish and there is a whole section with my favorite fish dishes.

I love cooking and baking and more than anything hope to pass on that passion through this book. Food connects people and so I invite you to connect with me and my family in the pages that follow.
Orly

About the Book and Cooking Philosophy

*My mother, who has been my biggest influence in the kitchen, taught me to improvise while cooking and that is how I recommend that you use my recipes. **Try them and then use them as a jumping off point to be inspired and make them your own.** Switch up the vegetables or change the spices to create your own flavors - there's no such thing as failure in the kitchen, only learning experiences. Of course baking is all about accuracy, but there's still room to play there as well. Change plums to peaches or hazelnuts to almonds and see what happens.*

As a trained nutritionist, my recipes emphasize healthy eating with lots of fresh fruits and vegetables, fish, grains, legumes and olive oil.

I rarely fry (except on Hanukkah when frying is a must!), I avoid butter and I rarely use fatty products. I prefer to make salad dressings, dough and bread from scratch and I hope to show readers not to be intimidated by this.

***The recipes in this book are very personal and reflect the way my family and I eat.** This book is a look into my home and my kitchen, a glimpse into my daily life and cooking classes. The recipes are inspired by my mother and grandmother, by newspaper clippings, by the shuk and by all the cultures that have come to Israel to make it the melting pot it is. They are largely inspired by the Sephardic cuisine that I grew up on and are* entirely kosher. In addition to simple, flavorful recipes that anyone can make, I've also included little tips and tricks to make cooking as easy as possible. These are things I've learned throughout the years from trial and error, fellow cooks and even my students.

Every recipe in the book has a photo to go along with it and many include step-by-step photos to illustrate the process. **The photographs were all taken in my home with no artificial additions or food styling tricks**. So you know what the finished product will look like and that you can get the same results in your kitchen.

These recipes have been tested again and again and approved by my family, students and friends. I'm confident that you'll enjoy the healthy, natural, homemade dishes in this cookbook **and hope they provide a tasty starting off point for recipes of your own...**

Eggplant and Tomatoes are so

popular year-round in Israel that they show up in every restaurant, cookbook and home kitchen in seemingly endless combinations. They are also favorites in my household and I've chosen some of my preferred preparations and techniques to inspire you. I could have included many, many more but my editor Katherine stopped me to make room for other recipes. I'll save them for my next book...

Baba Ghanoush | Eggplant Baladi | Eggplant with Tomato Sauce Turkish Style
Eggplant with Tomato Salsa | Eggplant Salad Greek Style | Eggplant with Bulgarian
Cheese | Eggplant Siniye | Sweet and Sour Eggplant | Eggplant, Pepper and Tomato
Salad | Shakshouka with Eggplant | Spicy Tomato Salad | Tomatoes Stuffed with Herbs
Cherry Tomato Salad with Basil and Feta

Baba Ghanoush
Eggplants with Tahini

While recipes for baba ghanoush - a Middle Eastern eggplant and tahini dip - are everywhere, the addition of yogurt is special. You can omit the yogurt to make traditional baba ghanoush, but it makes the dip super creamy and luscious.

2 medium eggplants

½ cup pure tahini

½ cup yogurt or buttermilk
(I prefer goat drinking yogurt)

Juice of 1 lemon, or more to taste

1-2 cloves garlic, finely chopped

Salt

Chopped parsley & mint

Olive oil

1. Grill the eggplants over a flame, turning with tongs until soft and evenly charred. Alternately, roast the eggplants under a broiler.

2. Cut a slit at the bottom of the eggplants and place in a sieve placed over a bowl. Leave to drain and reserve the liquid.

3. Once drained and cool enough to handle, remove the peel, stem and dark seeds.

4. Roughly chop the pulp.

5. In a large bowl, combine the tahini, yogurt, lemon juice, garlic, salt and some of the reserved eggplant liquid (taste first to make sure it is not too bitter) and mix well.

6. Add the eggplant pulp to the tahini mixture and mix thoroughly. Taste and season with additional lemon juice or salt as necessary.

7. Mix in some chopped parsley and mint.

8. Drizzle with olive oil and garnish with additional parsley and mint before serving.

TIP: When buying an eggplant, choose one that is relatively light for its size and has a very shiny skin.

Serves 4 to 6

Eggplant Baladi

I learned this recipe in a cooking class and it turned out to be a very successful dish with a surprising flavor combination. It is a wonderful use for date honey (called silan in Hebrew), which is very popular in the Israeli kitchen.

2 medium eggplants

2-3 cloves garlic, chopped

Sea salt

Juice of 1 lemon, or more to taste

3 Tbs. tahini

3 tsp. silan

Chopped parsley leaves

Pine nuts, toasted

Pomegranate seeds (in season)

1. Grill the eggplants over a flame, turning with tongs until soft and evenly charred. Alternately, roast the eggplants under a broiler.

2. Cut a slit at the bottom of the eggplants and place in a sieve. Leave to drain.

3. Remove peel, stem and dark seeds from eggplants and place on a plate or small serving platter.

4. Sprinkle the chopped garlic and sea salt over the eggplants then drizzle with lemon juice, tahini and silan.

5. Garnish with parsley, pine nuts and pomegranate seeds and serve.

TIP: *Remove the sprout in the center of each clove of garlic (called the "germ") to make it easier to digest.*

Serves 4 to 6

Eggplant with Tomato Sauce Turkish Style

The combination of eggplant and tomatoes was one that my mother used often in her cooking, so it feels natural to me. Although my mother didn't make her food very spicy, I like to add hot peppers. Many similar recipes call for frying the eggplant, but I prefer to bake it.

2 medium eggplants, cut into thick slices

Olive oil

3-4 Tbs. tomato paste

2-3 cloves garlic, chopped

3-4 tomatoes, diced

1-2 red hot peppers, sliced (optional)

Salt

Chopped parsley

1. Preheat the oven to 250°C/480°F.

2. Brush both sides of the eggplant slices with olive oil and put on a baking pan.

3. Bake for 20 minutes, until evenly browned.

4. Meanwhile, heat 2 tablespoons olive oil in a pan over medium heat. Add the tomato paste and stir for a few minutes. Add the garlic and diced tomatoes and simmer.

5. Transfer the baked eggplant into the tomato sauce. At this point you can add the red pepper as well. Season with salt.

6. Simmer the eggplants with the sauce about 20 minutes, until the tomatoes have cooked down and the sauce is slightly thickened.

7. Serve at room temperature. Garnish with chopped parsley just before serving.

Variation:

• If fresh tomatoes are not available or in season, use canned.

Serves 4 to 6

Roasted Eggplant with Tomato Salsa

Eggplant is immensely popular in Israeli cuisine and this dish is one of many that highlight the vegetable. Here, fresh lemon juice, tomatoes and cilantro provide the perfect contrast to the smoky roasted eggplant.

2 medium eggplants

2 tomatoes, chopped

2-3 cloves garlic, minced

½ cup finely chopped cilantro

Green hot pepper, chopped (optional)

Salt

Juice of 1 lemon, or more to taste

3 Tbs. tahini paste

½ cup canned or boiled chickpeas
(optional)

1. Roast the eggplants over an open flame or in the broiler until very soft and charred.

2. Cut a slit at the bottom of the eggplants and place in a sieve. Leave to drain.

3. Once drained and cool enough to handle, remove the peel and dark seeds (leave the stem on).

4. Put the tomatoes, garlic, cilantro, hot pepper and salt in a bowl and mix to combine.

5. Drizzle the eggplants with the lemon juice and tahini, then spoon the tomato mixture over.

6. Garnish with chickpeas, if using, and serve.

Serves 4 to 6

Eggplant Salad Greek Style

Every grocery store in Israel sells a salad like this. I prefer fresh cucumbers to pickled here as they give the salad a nice fresh flavor.

2 medium eggplants

1 small onion, diced

1-2 tomatoes, diced

1-2 fresh or pickled cucumbers, diced

1-2 cloves garlic, finely chopped

½ cup finely chopped parsley

Green hot pepper (optional)

1 avocado, diced (optional)

Juice of 1 lemon, or more to taste

Olive oil

Salt

1. Grill the eggplants over a flame, turning with tongs until soft and evenly charred. Alternately, roast the eggplants under a broiler.

2. Cut a slit at the bottom of the eggplants and place in a sieve. Leave to drain.

3. When cool enough to handle, remove the peel and rough seeds and roughly chop.

4. In a small bowl, mix together the onion, tomato, cucumbers, garlic, parsley, hot pepper, avocado and lemon juice with the chopped eggplant.

5. Season with olive oil and salt.

Serves 4 to 6

Eggplant with Bulgarian Cheese

Eggplant with feta is one of my favorite combinations and this recipe is an homage to my Greek heritage. Besides incorporating flavors I enjoy, it's also a colorful and beautiful dish that will complement any table.

1-2 eggplants

1 red pepper

Lemon juice

Salt & ground pepper

Bulgarian white cheese or feta, crumbled

Kalamata olives, pitted and chopped (optional)

1-2 cloves garlic, chopped (optional)

Olive oil

Mint & parsley leaves

1. Grill the eggplants and pepper over a flame, turning with tongs until soft and evenly charred. Alternately, roast under a broiler.

2. Cut a slit at the bottom of the eggplants and place in a sieve. Leave to drain.

3. Peel the burnt skin and remove dark seeds. Roughly chop the eggplant. Peel off the skin and slice the pepper.

4. Spread the eggplant on a plate and season with lemon juice, salt and pepper.

5. Top with the red pepper, cheese, olives and garlic, if using.

6. Drizzle lightly with olive oil and garnish with mint and parsley leaves.

7. Serve at room temperature.

Serves 4 to 6

Eggplant Siniye

Siniye is a typical Arab preparation in which the main ingredient is baked in tahini. Although it's most often made with minced meat, I prefer it with fish and eggplant. Eggplant is usually roasted, baked, or fried, but here it is steamed for a healthy, clean flavor.

2-3 eggplants, peeled

8 cherry tomatoes, halved
(optional)

⅔ cup tahini

1⅓ cups water

Juice of 1 lemon

2 cloves garlic, chopped

½ tsp. salt

2 onions, thinly sliced

¼ cup olive oil

Pine nuts, toasted

Chopped parsley

1. Heat the oven to 190°C/375°F.

2. Cut the eggplants in half, then cut each half into 4. Steam in a steamer for about 15 minutes.

3. Arrange the steamed eggplants in a baking pan. Nestle the cherry tomatoes, if using, amongst the eggplants.

4. Mix the tahini with the water, lemon juice, garlic and salt until it forms a diluted sauce.

5. Pour the tahini sauce on top of the eggplants.

6. Bake about 10 minutes, until the tahini thickens.

7. Meanwhile, fry the onions with the olive oil until caramelized. Set aside.

8. Spread the caramelized onions and pine nuts over the eggplant and bake for another 5 minutes.

9. Garnish with parsley just before serving. Serve at room temperature.

TIP: When caramelizing onions, add a few drops of water to the pan after they start to caramelize. This gets all the delicious browned and caramelized bits from the bottom without having to add more oil.

Serves 6

Sweet and Sour Eggplant

This is one of those dishes that I used to make all the time but then somehow forgot about. A friend reminded me of it when I visited her because she said that she makes it all the time. Now it's back in my regular rotation! Normally in a recipe like this the eggplant would be fried, but I try to be healthy and so bake the eggplant, which is very nice.

2 medium eggplants, cut into large cubes

Olive oil

2 onions, chopped

1-2 red peppers, chopped

3 Tbs. tomato paste

½ cup water

1 tsp. sweet paprika

½ tsp. hot paprika

Salt & pepper

⅓ cup vinegar

3 Tbs. sugar

Chopped parsley

Lemon zest (optional)

1. Preheat the oven to 250°C/480°F.

2. Put the eggplant pieces on a large, parchment-lined baking sheet and brush with olive oil. Bake for 20 minutes until lightly browned.

3. Meanwhile, fry the onions and peppers in olive oil until the onions are golden brown. Add the baked eggplant and cook for another few minutes, stirring occasionally.

4. In a small bowl, mix the tomato paste with the water, sweet and hot paprika, salt and pepper. Add to the vegetables, stir and cook covered for about 10 minutes.

5. Add the vinegar and sugar and allow to simmer, uncovered, for another few minutes.

6. Garnish with chopped parsley and lemon zest, if you like, before serving. Can be served hot or room temperature.

Serves 4 to 6

Eggplant, Pepper and Tomato Salad

This recipe, as with many of the eggplant recipes in this collection, introduces the flavor and technique of roasting eggplants and vegetables. It's immensely popular in Israel and a versatile technique to master.

1-2 eggplants

2 tomatoes

1-2 hot peppers (optional)

1 red pepper

1 green pepper

1 onion, peeled (optional)

3-4 Tbs. olive oil

3-4 Tbs. lemon juice

2-3 cloves garlic, chopped

Salt and ground pepper

1. Grill the eggplants, tomatoes, peppers and onion over a flame, turning with tongs until soft and evenly charred. Alternately, roast the vegetables under a broiler.

2. Put the peppers in a covered bowl to sweat (it helps to peel the skin). Cut a slit at the bottom of the eggplant and place in a sieve. Leave to drain.

3. Peel the skin of the vegetables, remove dark seeds and cut into chunky pieces.

4. Drizzle with the olive oil, lemon juice and chopped garlic. Season with salt and pepper.

TIP: *When chopping garlic, sprinkle it with a little salt. This will soften the garlic and make it easier to mince.*

Serves 4 to 6

Shakshuka with Eggplant

Shakshuka may have originated in Libya, but Israel has claimed it as its own. You can find it at every café, corner falafel or take away stand and home kitchen. Simply eggs poached in tomato sauce, I like to add eggplant to this comforting classic to give it even more heft. Be sure to serve it with plenty of bread or pita to sop up the delicious sauce.

2 eggplants

3-4 Tbs. olive oil

1 hot green pepper, sliced (optional)

4 cloves garlic, sliced

1 cup quartered cherry tomatoes

2 tomatoes, grated

Sea salt

4-6 eggs

Chopped parsley or cilantro

Crumbled feta cheese (optional)

1. Grill the eggplants over a flame, turning with tongs until soft and evenly charred. Alternately, roast the eggplants under a broiler.

2. Cut a slit at the bottom of the eggplant and place in a sieve. Leave to drain.

3. When cool enough to handle, remove the peel and rough seeds and roughly chop.

4. Heat the olive oil in a large sauté pan and fry the hot pepper (if using) until it gets dark. Add the garlic and roasted eggplant and cook for 1 minute.

5. Add the tomatoes and sea salt and simmer over high heat until the sauce thickens.

6. Break an egg into a small dish and gently slide it into the pan over the tomato sauce. Repeat with the remaining eggs, spacing them evenly apart.

7. Remove from the heat when the egg whites are set and the yolks still soft.

8. Sprinkle with parsley or cilantro and crumbled feta (if using) and serve with plenty of challah or other fresh bread.

Serves 4 to 6

Spicy Tomato Salad

This easy to make salad is an excellent addition to any mezze spread.It is also nice with fuul (page 126), falafel (page 122), or even spooned over fish. You can adjust the amount of hot pepper you add to suit your tastes.

4 tomatoes, chopped

1 hot green pepper, sliced

1-2 cloves garlic, minced

½ bunch cilantro, chopped

1-2 pieces preserved lemon, chopped (substitute lemon zest)

2-3 Tbs. olive oil

2-3 Tbs. lemon juice

Salt & pepper

½ tsp. cumin (optional)

1. Put the tomatoes, hot pepper, garlic, cilantro and preserved lemon in a bowl.

2. Dress well with olive oil and lemon juice and season with salt, pepper and cumin, if using.

Serves 4 to 6

Tomatoes Stuffed with Herbs

I came up with this dish because I was looking for a lighter stuffed vegetable recipe that didn't use rice. You can serve it as a side, at brunch, or even for a light supper along with a salad.

6 tomatoes, halved

1 tsp. brown sugar

Salt

4 Tbs. olive oil

1 cup finely chopped parsley

½ cup finely chopped basil or mint leaves

1 Tbs. fresh thyme

½ cup breadcrumbs

1 clove garlic, minced

Pepper

Grated Parmesan cheese (optional)

1. Preheat the oven to 190°C/375°F.

2. Cut each tomato in half and use a small spoon to scoop out the pulp and seeds.

3. Coarsely chop the tomato pulp and mix with the sugar, salt and 2 tablespoons of the olive oil.

4. Spoon the tomato and sugar mixture into a large baking pan.

5. In a separate bowl, mix together the herbs, breadcrumbs, garlic, salt, pepper and the remaining 2 tablespoons olive oil.

6. Stuff the tomatoe with the herb and breadcrumbs mixture and place them on top of the sauce in the baking pan.

7. Sprinkle with Parmesan cheese, if using.

8. Bake for 30 minutes, until the breadcrumbs are lightly browned.

9. Remove from the oven and drizzle with olive oil before serving.

Variation:

- Replace the breadcrumbs with fine bulgur. Soak ⅓ cup bulgur in ⅓ cup boiling water, then continue with the recipe as directed.

Serves 8 to 12

Cherry Tomato Salad with Basil and Feta

One of my favorite flavor combinations is tomato with Bulgarian (feta) cheese and basil and olive oil only improves it. It's my Israeli version on the classic Italian tomato and mozzarella combination. This is so simple to make and you can make it just for one or for a crowd. I leave the measurements up to you.

Assorted cherry tomatoes, halved

Feta cheese, crumbled

Basil leaves

Drizzle of good extra virgin olive oil

1. Toss all the ingredients together and serve!

Serves 4 to 6

Salads

Nearly every meal in Israel - even breakfast - is enjoyed with a salad. The popularity of salad is a testament to the freshness of the produce here and people make them at home and eat them out. Every family has their own variations, mixing together whatever vegetables, fruits, nuts, grains and cheeses are freshest. In a way, Israeli cuisine is like one big tossed salad.

Raw Beet and Apple Salad | Orange and Fennel Salad | Cabbage Salad for Falafel
Cabbage and Cranberry Salad | Purple Cabbage Salad | Carrot and Pecan Salad
Israeli Salad with Pomegranate and Avocado | Green Salad with Strawberries
The President's Salad | Parsley, Nuts & Feta Cheese Salad | White Bean Salad
Multicolor Pepper Antipasti

Raw Beet and Apple Salad

I tasted a salad with beets and apples and loved it so much that I started making my own. I added celery and walnuts for added flavor and crunch. I want to inspire people to use fresh, raw beets - you don't need to cook them or anything!

For the Salad:

1-2 beets, peeled and grated

2 green apples, grated

1-2 stalks celery, chopped

Chopped walnuts (optional)

For the Dressing:

2 tsp. silan (date honey)

Lemon juice

1-2 Tbs. balsamic vinegar

Sea salt

1. Put all the salad ingredients in a large bowl and toss to combine.

2. In a separate bowl, whisk together the silan, lemon juice to taste, balsamic vinegar and salt. Pour over the salad and toss again.

Variation:

• Add grated ginger to the salad to brighten the flavor even more.

Serves 4 to 6

Orange and Fennel Salad

The combination of fruits and vegetables in salads is very Israeli. Oranges, in particular, are identified with Israel and this recipe pairs them with fennel for an unusual flavor pairing. A variation of this combination exists also in Moroccan and Greek cuisine.

2 oranges

½ cup kalamata or oil-cured black olives, pitted and chopped

1 small red onion, thinly sliced

1-2 bulbs fennel, sliced

½ cup torn basil and/or mint leaves

2 Tbs. olive oil

2-3 Tbs. lemon juice

2 Tbs. silan (date honey)

1. Peel the oranges and trim away any remaining white pith. Chop into bite-sized pieces.

2. Put the oranges, olives, red onion, fennel and basil and/or mint in a bowl and toss gently to combine.

3. In a separate bowl, whisk together the olive oil, lemon juice and silan.

4. Drizzle over the salad and toss to thoroughly coat. Serve immediately.

Serves 4

Cabbage Salad for Falafel

*You'll find a similar vegetable salad at every falafel stand across Israel.
It's perfect stuffed in a pita with falafel (page 122) or shawarma, but it's
also excellent on its own or as a side.*

¼ white cabbage, shredded

Salt

2 tomatoes, cut into cubes

2 cucumbers, cut into cubes

½ cup roughly chopped
fresh mint

Olive oil

Lemon juice

Cumin (optional)

Sumac (optional)

1. Put the cabbage in a large bowl and sprinkle liberally with rough salt. Massage it with your hands until the cabbage has softened.

2. Add the tomatoes, cucumbers and mint and toss to combine.

3. In a separate bowl, whisk together the olive oil, lemon juice, cumin, sumac and additional salt.

4. Pour the dressing over the salad and toss.

Serves 4 to 6

Cabbage and Cranberry Salad

I found a similar recipe in the newspaper and was inspired to make my own.
I loved it and have been making it since. Whenever I share it with friends
and family they rave about it, so I'm sharing it here.

½ head white cabbage, shredded

1 tsp. salt

¼ cup freshly squeezed lemon juice

2 Tbs. canola oil

3-4 Tbs. brown sugar

2 Tbs. vinegar

Chopped cilantro

½ cup cranberries

1. Put the shredded cabbage in a large bowl.

2. Add the salt and lemon juice and toss with your hands, massaging the cabbage until it has softened slightly.

3. Add the canola oil, sugar, vinegar, cilantro and cranberries and toss to combine.

4. Serve immediately or store in a covered container in the refrigerator for up to two days.

Serves 4 to 6

Purple Cabbage Salad

Covering the cabbage with hot water is an easy way to soften it without overcooking.
The acid in the lemon juice causes the cabbage to turn a vibrant hot pink,
making it a gorgeous addition to any table.

½ red cabbage, shredded

⅓ cup olive oil or canola oil

⅓ cup freshly squeezed lemon juice or vinegar

2 tsp. salt

2 Tbs. brown sugar

1. Put the shredded cabbage in a large, heatproof bowl and cover with boiling water. Let it sit until the water has cooled, then drain. Return the cabbage to the bowl.

2. Add the remaining ingredients and toss to combine. Allow to rest for a little bit before serving.

Serves 4 to 6

Carrot and Pecan Salad

This salad is so simple, but so delicious. It goes well with just about any meal and best of all can be made ahead. The flavors only improve.

4-5 carrots, peeled

1 bunch chives or spring onion, chopped

1 cup sweet pecans, roughly chopped

3 Tbs. canola oil

¼ cup vinegar (white or red wine, white balsamic, or apple cider vinegar are all good choices)

1 Tbs. mustard

2 Tbs. demerara or brown sugar

1 clove garlic, minced (optional)

1. Grate the carrots on the medium side of a box grater and put them in a salad bowl. Add the chives and pecans.

2. In a separate bowl, whisk together the canola oil, vinegar, mustard, sugar and garlic, if using.

3. Pour the dressing over the salad and toss until fully coated.

4. Serve immediately or store in a covered container in the fridge until ready to eat.

Serves 4 to 6

Israeli Salad with Pomegranate and Avocado

The basic Israeli salad, which is simply chopped tomatoes and cucumbers, is served with every meal at every time of day in Israel. This is my dressed up version with radish, avocado, mint and pomegranate seeds. One past student wrote to tell me, "I have served your salad with the pomegranate seeds with rave reviews. It is a flavor and texture most are not familiar with and was liked by all."

1-2 tomatoes, cut into cubes

1-2 cucumbers cut into cubes

1-2 radishes, cut into strips

1 avocado, cut into cubes

½ cup roughly chopped mint

Pomegranate seeds (optional)

Chopped preserved lemon (optional)

Lemon juice

Olive oil

Salt

Sumac

1. Put the tomatoes, cucumbers, radishes, avocado, mint, pomegranate seeds and preserved lemon in a large bowl and toss to combine.

2. Whisk together lemon juice, olive oil, salt and sumac to taste and toss with the salad. Garnish with additional pomegranate seeds and serve.

Serves 4 to 6

Green Salad with Strawberries

Ramat Hasharon, where I live, was famous for its strawberry fields. Now only a few remain and I love being able to get fresh, local strawberries just a few minutes from my home. While strawberries are a summer fruit in many parts of the world, here they peak in winter. I love how this bright salad highlights the fruit and people go nuts for it every time I serve it.

For the Salad:

2 cups mixed lettuce leaves

2 cups spinach leaves

1 basket strawberries, hulled and halved

½ cup sweet pecans

For the Dressing:

⅓ cup balsamic vinegar

⅓ cup silan (date honey)

½ tsp. salt

1¼ cup vegetable oil

1. Mix all the lettuce and spinach leaves together in a salad bowl.

2. Sprinkle the strawberries and pecans on top.

3. To make the dressing, mix all the ingredients with a hand blender or in a food processor until smooth. Season before serving. (This makes plenty of extra dressing, but it's excellent on any salad and will keep for at least a week in the fridge.)

4. Drizzle the dressing over the salad and serve.

Serves 6 to 8

The President's Salad

The inspiration for this salad came from a recipe in the newspaper by the Israeli president's chef. Lettuce, oranges and pomegranates are a classic Mediterranean combination and I was drawn to these ingredients. It would be perfect for Tu Bishvat.

2 oranges

½ cup pomegranate seeds

¼ cup roughly chopped walnuts

2-3 cups lettuce leaves

½ cup arugula

2 Tbs. olive oil

2 Tbs. lemon juice

Pinch of salt

Dash of honey or silan (optional)

1. Peel the oranges and trim away any remaining white pith. Break apart into segments.

2. Put the orange segments, pomegranate seeds, walnuts, lettuce and arugula into a salad bowl and toss with olive oil, lemon juice and a pinch of salt. Add a drizzle of honey or silan if you prefer a sweeter dressing.

Serves 4 to 6

Parsley, Nuts & Feta Cheese Salad

This salad always surprises people. While parsley and other fresh herbs are typically used as a garnish, here they take center stage in a fresh and flavorful salad. The cashews and feta give this otherwise light salad a welcome touch of richness.

½ bunch parsley, chopped

½ bunch cilantro or basil, chopped

½ bunch mint, chopped

½ cup almond slivers, toasted

½ cup cashew nuts, toasted

100 g (3½ oz) feta cheese, diced

¼ cup olive oil

Juice of 1 lemon

Sumac

1. Put the parsley, cilantro, mint, almond, cashews and feta in a bowl and mix.

2. Whisk together the olive oil, lemon juice and sumac and pour over the salad. Toss to coat.

Serves 4 to 6

White Bean Salad

This is a very Greek recipe. You can substitute any other kind of large, dry beans for the white ones here.

½-1 cup large, dried white beans

1 small red onion, chopped

1-2 cloves garlic, chopped

1 hot chili, sliced (substitute chili flakes)

Kalamata olives, chopped (optional)

¼ cup olive oil

3-4 Tbs. red wine vinegar or lemon juice

Coarse salt & pepper

Chopped parsley

1. Put the beans in large bowl or pot and cover with plenty of water. Soak overnight.

2. The next day, drain the beans then put in a large pot of fresh water. Simmer for 1 to 2 hours, until soft.

3. In a bowl, mix the beans, onion, garlic, chili, olives, oil, vinegar, salt and pepper. Toss to combine and garnish with parsley. Serve immediately, if you wish, but it's even better the next day.

Serves 4 to 6

Multicolor Pepper Antipasti

*This is something that my mother used to make often. I use balsamic vinegar,
which isn't particularly Israeli and wasn't an ingredient that my mother used,
but I love the way it tastes with the roasted peppers.*

6 assorted sweet peppers

2-3 tsp. olive oil

Balsamic vinegar or lemon juice

1-2 cloves garlic, thinly sliced

Fresh thyme or oregano

Salt & pepper

1. Arrange the peppers in a baking dish and roast or broil until charred.

2. Remove from the oven and put in a covered bowl so the skin can sweat.

3. Peel off the skin, remove all the seeds and cut the peppers into strips (or, for a different presentation, roughly chop).

4. Season with the olive oil, balsamic vinegar or lemon juice, garlic, thyme, salt and pepper. Serve at room temperature.

Serves 6 to 8

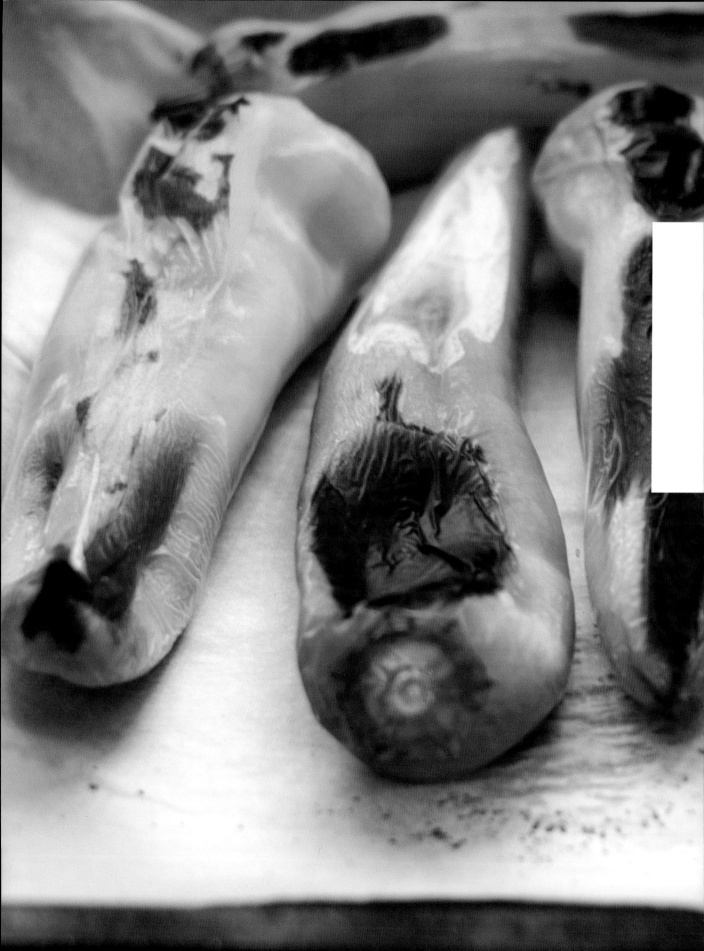

Fresh **Vegetables** *are in abundance in Israel and my guests always tell me that the vegetables here taste unbelievably delicious. It's true! As a vegetarian of many years I use lots of vegetables in my daily cooking. And as a nutritionist I know how good they are for you!*

Stuffed Peppers with Cheese | Stuffed Peppers with Rice | Okra with Yogurt Sauce Zucchini in Yogurt Sauce | Green Beans in Tomato Sauce | Pumpkin Stew with Carrots and Raisins | Roasted Cauliflower with Tahini and Silan | Spinach Pie Green Shakshuka | Swiss Chard with Rice | Onion Tart | Preserved Lemons | Zhug

Stuffed Peppers with Rice

Stuffed vegetables are hugely popular in Israel and this is a dish that you can find at workingman restaurants and Shabbat tables across the country. On Fridays we can smell it cooking throughout our building. I prefer small peppers for stuffing as opposed to the large ones.

6-8 assorted sweet peppers

For the Filling:

1 cup Persian rice

3 Tbs. olive oil

1 onion, chopped

Salt & pepper

½ cup chopped parsley

1 tsp. ras-el-hanout

½ cup pine nuts, toasted (optional)

For the Sauce:

500 g (1 lb) tomatoes, grated
(substitute canned tomatoes)

2 cups boiling water

1 cup beer or white wine

2 Tbs. sugar (optional)

Salt & pepper

1 Tbs. sweet paprika

½ Tbs. hot paprika (optional)

1. Prepare the peppers: Cut the caps (reserve) and remove the seeds.

2. Rinse the rice and soak it in lukewarm water for 20 minutes.

3. Heat the olive oil in a large pan and fry onions until translucent.

4. Add the rice, salt and pepper and cook for a few more minutes.

5. Remove from the heat and stir in the parsley, ras-el-hanout and pine nuts (if using).

6. Fill the peppers with the rice mixture and arrange in a pot.

7. Mix together the sauce ingredients and pour over the peppers. Cover with the reserved caps.

8. Cook over low heat, covered, for about 1 hour. Remove from the heat and serve.

Variation:

- Instead of 1 cup rice in the filling, use ½ cup rice with 500g (1 lb) ground meat or 1 cup cooked lentils.

Serves 6 to 8

Stuffed Peppers with Cheese

This recipe is typical of the Balkans and something I learned to make from my mother. The salty cheese is a nice contrast to the sweet peppers and the presentation is quite pretty.

8 assorted long, sweet peppers

250 g (9 oz) quark or ricotta cheese

100 g (3½ oz) feta or Bulgarian cheese

1 large or 2 small eggs, lightly beaten

1 Tbs. olive oil, plus more for drizzling

1-2 Tbs. breadcrumbs

1. Preheat the oven to 180°C/350°F.

2. Arrange the peppers in a baking dish and roast until slightly charred.

3. Put in a bowl and cover until cool enough to handle.

4. Remove the skin from each pepper, cut a slit lengthwise and remove the seeds.

5. Mix together the ricotta, feta, eggs, olive oil and breadcrumbs. Spoon the filling into the peppers and arrange so they fit snugly in a baking dish.

6. Drizzle with olive oil and bake for 30 to 40 minutes, until the cheese is bubbly. Remove from the oven and serve.

Okra with Yogurt Sauce

Okra, called "bamia" in Hebrew, is a very popular vegetable in Sephardic and Arabic kitchens. My mother used to make it in tomato sauce (see the recipe for green beans in tomato sauce, page 80), but this version with yogurt was inspired by Arabic cuisine, which uses a lot of yogurt in cooking. If possible use small okra, which are more flavorful.

500 g (1 lb) fresh or frozen small okra

2 Tbs. olive oil

1-2 cloves garlic

Juice of 1 lemon

Salt

Yogurt

Mint leaves

1. Trim the stems of the okra, but not all the way to the end.

2. Heat oil in a large pan and fry the garlic.

3. Add the okra to the pan and fry for 2 to 3 minutes, stirring often. (Frying the okra keeps it dry and prevents it from becoming slimy.)

4. Add lemon juice to the pan and simmer for a few more minutes, until okra softens. Season with salt and remove from the heat.

5. To serve, fill a small serving bowl with yogurt and pile the cooked okra on top. Drizzle lightly with olive oil and garnish with mint leaves.

TIP: Watch the garlic carefully while frying as it burns easily and becomes bitter.

Serves 4 to 6

Zucchini in Yogurt Sauce

Cooking yogurt is an Arabic technique that I've picked up and one that I really like. I learned this particular dish from an Arab cook in the Galilee and I just love the flavors. While it's not the prettiest dish on the table, it makes up for its humble looks with a wonderful, unusual taste.

2 white onions, diced

¼ cup olive oil

6 zucchini, diced or thickly sliced

1 Tbs. salt

1 liter yogurt

1. Fry the onions in olive oil until caramelized.

2. Add the zucchini and cook, stirring occasionally, for about 25 minutes.

3. Stir in the salt.

4. Meanwhile, in a separate pan, cook the yogurt over medium heat, stirring constantly, until has reduced and can coat the back of a spoon.

5. Add the yogurt to the zucchini and stir until the zucchini is fully coated. Serve immediately.

Serves 4 to 6

Green Beans in Tomato Sauce

My mother used to make this all the time, but she typically used okra. Yellow beans or zucchini work as well in this versatile dish. It is an excellent side dish for almost any meal and I particularly like it with rice.

2 Tbs. olive or canola oil

1 onion, chopped

1-2 cloves garlic, chopped

1 tsp. turmeric

500 g (½ lb) fresh or frozen green beans, trimmed

2 tomatoes, diced or grated
(substitute canned tomatoes)

2 Tbs. tomato paste

1 tsp. sugar (optional)

Salt & pepper

1. Heat the oil in a large skillet and fry the onion, garlic and turmeric.

2. Add the green beans and fry for another 2 to 3 minutes.

3. Add the tomatoes, tomato paste, sugar and enough water to just cover the beans.

4. Cook, covered, until the sauce has thickened and the green beans are tender.

5. Season with salt and pepper and serve.

TIP: If you don't want to add sugar, sauté the tomato paste for a few minutes before adding the tomatoes and water. It will caramelize slightly, allowing you to omit the sugar.

Serves 4 to 6

Pumpkin Stew with Carrots and Raisins

This is one of those dishes that I prepared for a cooking class and it was such a big hit that I've kept it in my rotation. It's sweet and savory with a distinct flavor that is perfect for autumn.

300 g (10½ oz) pumpkin, diced

2-3 carrots, sliced

Vegetable oil

2 onions, sliced

150 g (about ¾ cup) golden raisins

1 cup cooked chickpeas (optional)

1-2 Tbs. sugar

½ tsp. cinnamon

¼ tsp. ground cloves

Salt

1. Cook the pumpkin and carrots separately in boiling water until soft but not mushy.

2. Meanwhile, heat vegetable oil in a large skillet and sauté the onions until golden.

3. Add the pumpkin, carrots, raisins, chickpeas, sugar, cinnamon, cloves and a little water and cook, uncovered, for 10 to 15 minutes.

4. Season with salt and serve with couscous.

Serves 4 to 6

Roasted Cauliflower with Tahini and Silan

I've made a similar recipe with eggplant for a long time (see eggplant baladi, page 20), but someone at one of my cooking classes didn't like eggplant . So I came up with this variation instead to highlight the flavor combination and show people unexpected ways to use silan (date honey).

1 cauliflower, cut into florets

¼ cup olive oil

Sea salt

Lemon juice

2-3 Tbs. tahini

2-3 tsp. silan (date honey)

Chopped parsley

Pomegranate seeds (in season) or dried cranberries

Toasted pine nuts

1. Preheat the oven to 200°C/400°F.

2. Put the cauliflower florets in a baking dish (preferably one that you can serve with). Don't worry if the cauliflower is piled high or the dish looks too small since the cauliflower shrinks a lot as it cooks. Toss with the olive oil and sprinkle with salt.

3. Roast until the cauliflower is tender (when your fingernail can easily enter) and the edges have browned, 15 to 20 minutes. Remove from the oven and allow to cool slightly.

4. Arrange the cauliflower on a serving plate. Drizzle with lemon juice, tahini and silan, in that order.

5. Garnish with chopped parsley, pomegranate seeds or cranberries and pine nuts and serve.

Serves 4 to 6

Moroccan Carrot Salad

This is a hugely popular salad in Israel and can be found in many restaurants and homes.
It makes a lovely cold side dish that complements meat and vegetarian dishes alike.
I leave the exact measurements of the spices and lemon juice to your taste buds;
play around until the salad is to your liking.

3-4 carrots

Olive oil

Lemon juice

1 clove garlic, minced

Salt & pepper

Hot paprika

Cumin

Chopped parsley leaves

1. Put the whole carrots in a pot of water and boil until tender but not mushy.

2. Drain, peel and slice the carrots into coins.

3. Put in a bowl and season with olive oil, lemon juice, garlic, salt, pepper, hot paprika, cumin and parsley to taste.

Serves 4 to 6

Spinach Pie

My mother used spinach a lot in her cooking. She filled borekas with the leafy green, made patties and prepared this delicious savory pie. Similar to a crustless quiche, this dish is excellent for breakfast or lunch or as a side dish and is good hot or room temperature.

1 kg (2.2 lbs) spinach

1 boiled potato

200 g (7 oz) feta or Bulgarian cheese, crumbled

50 g (1¾ oz) kashkaval, grated
(substitute caciocavallo or provolone)

2 eggs

1 Tbs. olive oil

Nutmeg

1. Preheat the oven to 180°C/350°F.

2. Blanche the spinach in a pot of boiling water for 3 to 4 minutes. Drain and rinse with cold water.

3. Squeeze out as much liquid as possible and roughly chop.

4. Mash the boiled potato.

5. Mix together the chopped spinach, mashed potato, cheeses and eggs. Add the olive oil and a pinch of nutmeg.

6. Transfer to a 20x30-cm baking pan and bake for 40 to 50 minutes, until the top is golden brown.

TIP: Instead of boiling a potato, prick it with a fork a few times, moisten it, and put it in the microwave for about 2 minutes per side.

Serves 8 to 10

Green Shakshuka

This version of shakshuka can be found in Israeli cafés and restaurants for those who want a change of pace from regular shakshuka. The color is great, as is the taste - especially with fresh bread on the side.

3-4 Tbs. olive oil

1 onion, diced

3-4 cloves garlic, minced

1-2 spring onions, sliced (optional)

1 bunch Swiss chard, roughly chopped (leaves and stalks separated)

1 bunch spinach leaves, roughly chopped

2 Tbs. white wine

½ cup heavy cream

Salt & pepper

Nutmeg

4-6 eggs

Feta cheese, crumbled (optional)

1. Heat olive oil in a large skillet and sauté the onion, garlic, spring onions and Swiss chard stalks until the onions are golden brown.

2. Add the spinach and Swiss chard leaves. Cook for a few minutes, stirring, until the leaves lose half of their volume.

3. Stir in the wine and cream and season with salt, pepper and a pinch of nutmeg.

4. Bring to a boil and lower the heat. Cook for 20 minutes on low heat.

5. Break an egg into a small dish and gently slide into the pan. Repeat with remaining eggs, evenly spacing them within the pan.

6. Cover and cook until the egg whites are set but the yolks are still soft (or to your preference).

7. Remove the lid, sprinkle with cheese, if using and serve with plenty of fresh bread.

Serves 4 to 6

Swiss Chard with Rice

My mother used to make rice with spinach and lemon juice and this is similar. The hot paprika and cilantro, two ingredients that my mother never used, are what give this dish Moroccan flare. I learned the taste of cilantro from my in-laws.

¼ cup olive oil

2 onions, chopped

½ kg (1 lb) Swiss chard, chopped (stems & leaves)

½ cup chopped cilantro

1 tsp. sweet paprika

½ tsp. hot paprika

¼ cup water

½ cup rice

½ cup cooked chickpeas (optional)

Salt & pepper

1. Heat the olive oil in a large pan and fry the onions, Swiss chard, cilantro and sweet and hot paprika.

2. Add the water and bring to a boil. Cover and cook for about 20 minutes.

3. Add the rice and chickpeas and cook, covered, until the rice is tender. Add a spoonful of boiling water if necessary.

4. Season with salt and pepper and stir well. Serve immediately.

Serves 4 to 6

Onion Tart

This onion tart is my son's favorite. The onions get quite sweet, which pairs wonderfully with the thyme. It's very easy to prepare and since it contains protein-rich cheese and eggs it makes a wonderful light meal served with a salad.

Olive oil & butter

4-5 white and/or red onions, sliced

1 tsp. salt

1 tsp. fresh thyme (or ½ tsp. dry)

1 sheet puff pastry, defrosted

2 eggs

1 cup milk or heavy cream

1 cup grated Cheddar cheese

1. Preheat the oven to 200°C/400°F.

2. Heat some olive oil and butter in a pan and fry the onions until transparent.

3. Add salt and thyme and mix well.

4. Place the puff pastry dough in a greased rectangular baking dish. Arrange the onions on top of the dough.

5. Mix the eggs, milk and cheese and pour over the onions.

6. Bake until lightly browned and crisp.

7. Slice and serve.

*TIP: To cut an onion without crying, keep the root on until the end. One of my guests wrote on TripAdvisor: "Orly showed me how to cut an onion without tearing up. **This is a 'life-changer'!**".*

Serves 6 to 8

Preserved Lemons

Preserved lemons are a common ingredient in Middle Eastern and North African cooking and provide a wonderful tart, tangy flavor. You can make as much or as little as you want and the quantities will depend on the size of your jar.

Lemons (ones with a thin skin are preferable)

Kosher salt

Chili flakes (optional)

Freshly squeezed lemon juice

Olive oil

1. Slice or dice the lemons with the skin.

2. Sprinkle salt and chili flakes (if using) on top.

3. Put them in a sterilized jar so they fit snugly.

4. Pour lemon juice almost to cover, then pour olive oil to cover the lemons completely.

5. Tightly close the jar and leave at room temperature for about 1 week before opening.

6. After opening store in the refrigerator.

Zhug

This Yemenite hot sauce is immensely popular in Israel and can be found in every grocery store and at every falafel stand. Often it's just referred to as "harif," which means spicy in Hebrew.

4-5 hot green peppers, seeds removed

4 cloves garlic

½ tsp. cumin

1 bunch fresh cilantro

Salt

Lemon juice

1 slice preserved lemon
(optional)

1. Mix all the ingredients in a blender, food processor, immersion blender, or mortar and pestle.

2. If the mixture is too dry, add a teaspoon of water. Otherwise, serve immediately or store in a sealed container in the fridge for up to 1 week.

Grains and Legumes

are essential ingredients in my vegetarian kitchen and are a cornerstone of Israeli cuisine. I use rice, bulgur, lentils, chickpeas and more in many combinations and inspired by all the different cultures that contribute to the Israeli melting pot. From Arab mejadra to Iraqi kitchry, and from tabouleh to hummus, I put my own spin on each of these dishes that make good use of pantry staples.

Bulgur and Tomato Salad | Kitchry - Rice with Red Lentils Iraqi Style | Mejadra with Bulgur | Mejadra with Rice | Rice with Turmeric and Cinnamon | Hashwa - Rice with Meat | Sirknize - Bulgur with Chickpeas | Makluba - Upside Down Rice | Tabouleh Bukharan Chickpea Pastry | Falafel | Hummus | Fuul

Bulgur and Tomato Salad

Sometimes called burghul, bulgur is an excellent, fiber-rich whole grain to add to your diet. In this salad, cooked and raw tomatoes complement the bulgur for a dish that can be served warm or cold, as a side or light meal.

½ cup fine bulgur

⅓ cup water

Olive oil

1 small onion, chopped

1 Tbs. coriander seeds

3 tomatoes, cubed

2 spring onions, sliced

2 slices preserved lemon, chopped
(optional)

Salt

Chopped cilantro

1. Put the bulgur in a bowl and cover with the water. Soak until the water has been fully absorbed.

2. Meanwhile, fry the onion in olive oil until softened. Add half of the tomatoes and the coriander seeds and simmer for a few minutes. Pour on top of the bulgur.

3. Add the remaining fresh tomato, spring onions and preserved lemon, if using and season with salt.

4. Allow to sit so the flavors can meld for at least 30 minutes before serving. Can be served hot or cold.

5. Garnish with chopped cilantro and serve.

TIP: *Lightly crush the coriander seeds so they will open a bit for more flavor.*

Serves 4 to 6

Kitchry - Rice with Red Lentils Iraqi Style

This comforting rice and lentil dish is common in Iraqi families. I originally learned how to make it from my next door neighbor who was Iraqi and an accomplished home cook. After learning the basic technique from her I refined my own version. I added the onion because I wanted to show my cooking classes how to chop an onion and it turned out to be a great addition.

4 Tbs. vegetable oil

1-2 onions, chopped

1 tsp. turmeric

2 Tbs. tomato paste

1 cup white rice

½ cup red lentils

2 cups water

Salt

4-5 cloves garlic, minced

1 Tbs. ground cumin

Butter

1. Heat 2 tablespoons oil in a large sauté pan. Fry the chopped onion and turmeric until the onion is softened.

2. Add the tomato paste, rice, lentils and water.

3. Simmer, covered, until the water is absorbed. Remove from the heat and set aside.

4. In a separate large pan, heat the remaining 2 tablespoons oil. Fry the chopped garlic with the cumin until softened and aromatic; be careful not to burn the garlic and cumin.

5. Season the cooked rice and lentils with salt and add to the garlic and cumin. Sprinkle a few pats of butter across the top, cover and cook for a few minutes until the butter is melted and the bottom becomes a little crispy.

6. Uncover and flip the mixture as best as you can to get a nice, crispy crust all around.

7. Remove from the heat and serve.

Serves 6 to 8

Mejadra with Rice

This Middle Eastern dish is very popular in lots of homes in Israel. It can be served with a dollop of yogurt on top, tahini sauce (page 126), or with a salad to make it a light meal. Plus, it's naturally gluten free!

1 cup white rice

1 cup black and/or brown lentils

¼ cup olive oil

2-3 onions, chopped

1 tsp. cumin

1 tsp. salt

1. Soak the rice in cold tap water for about 30 minutes. Drain and set aside.

2. Soak the lentils in boiling water for about 15 minutes.

3. Drain the lentils and put them in a wide-rimmed pan over medium heat. Cover with water, cover and cook until the lentils are tender (water should only just cover the lentils; you can always add more if you need).

4. Meanwhile, heat the olive oil in a skillet and fry the onions until caramelized. Reserve some for garnishing.

5. Add the rice, caramelized onions and cumin to the lentils, stir and cover with water once again. Simmer, covered, for 20 minutes, until the water has absorbed.

6. Remove from the heat and let sit in the covered pan for another 10 minutes.

7. Add salt and stir well. Garnish with the reserved caramelized onions and serve.

TIP: *See page 30.*

Serves 6

Mejadra with Bulgur

While mejadra with rice is more common, this is more of a Druze-style dish from the Galilee. Because it uses bulgur it has a slightly different cooking method than traditional mejadra. It's easy to make, very healthy since it's a complete protein and would be a great choice for Meatless Mondays.

½ cup coarse bulgur

1 cup black and/or brown lentils

¼ cup olive oil

1-2 onions, chopped

1 tsp. sugar (optional)

1 tsp. salt

Pepper

1. Soak the bulgur in water for about 15 minutes. Drain and set aside.

2. In a separate bowl, soak the lentils in boiling water for about 15 minutes. Drain and set aside.

3. Meanwhile, heat the olive oil in a large skillet and fry the onions with the sugar (if using) until caramelized.

4. Add the drained lentils to the onions and pour over just enough water to cover. Cover and cook over low heat until the lentils are soft, about 20 minutes.

5. Add the bulgur and cook, covered, for a few more minutes until the water is fully absorbed.

6. Remove from the heat and let sit in the covered pan for another 5 minutes.

7. Add salt and pepper and stir well. Serve warm or at room temperature.

Serves 4 to 6

Rice with Turmeric and Cinnamon

This recipe was inspired by one I found in an Indian cookbook years ago.
I really like Indian food and this quickly became my rice recipe for the holidays.
The turmeric turns the rice a beautiful shade of yellow and it seems to go
with just about everything.

1 cup basmati rice

1½-2 cups water

1 tsp. turmeric

½ cinnamon stick, broken into pieces

3-4 cloves

2 bay leaves

Salt

2 Tbs. canola oil or butter

1. Put the rice, water, turmeric, broken cinnamon stick, cloves and bay leaves in a pot and simmer, covered, until done.

2. Remove the cinnamon sticks, cloves and bay leaves and discard.

3. Season with salt to taste and stir in the canola oil or butter and serve.

Serves 4 to 6

Hashwa - Rice with Meat

I found a recipe for this Arab dish somewhere and thought it sounded good. I tried it and everyone liked it, so I added it to the rotation. It's a big hit with my family. The aroma from the spices is wonderful and fills the whole house.

2-3 onions, chopped

Olive Oil

500 g (1 lb) ground beef

Salt and pepper

1-2 tsp. Baharat or ras el hanout or mix of paprika, cumin, ground cloves & cinnamon

1 cup white rice

Small handful golden raisins (optional)

2 cups boiling water

Toasted pine nuts

1. Fry the onions in olive oil in a large skillet over medium heat until softened.

2. Add the ground beef and cook, stirring often to break up the meat, until browned and crumbly.

3. Season with salt and pepper and stir in 1 tsp. of the spices. Add the rice and stir for 2 to 3 minutes.

4. Add the raisins, water and more spices if you like.

5. Bring to a boil and cook, covered, for 20 minutes at a simmer.

6. Turn off the heat and leave in the covered pan for another 20 minutes.

7. Sprinkle with pine nuts before serving.

serves 6 to 8

Sirknize - Bulgur with Chickpeas and Carrots

This dish from the Bukharan kitchen is usually made with rice, but I enjoy preparing it with bulgur (burghul). It makes a wonderful side, but is also hearty enough to make a light meal.

1 cup coarse bulgur (burghul) or rice

5 Tbs. olive oil

2 onions, chopped

2-3 carrots, diced

½ cup cooked or canned chickpeas

½ hot green or red pepper, sliced

2 cloves garlic, chopped

1 tsp. cumin

1 tsp. salt

½ cup chopped cilantro

1. Soak the bulgur in water for about 15 minutes. Drain and set aside.

2. Heat 3 tablespoons of the olive oil in a pan and add the onions. Cook over medium-low heat, stirring only occasionally, until caramelized.

3. Add the carrots, chickpeas and hot pepper and cook for 3 to 4 minutes.

4. Add the bulgur and water to cover.

5. Cook on low heat, covered, until the water is absorbed.

6. Turn off the heat and leave in the pan for another 5 minutes.

7. Meanwhile, fry chopped garlic and cumin in the remaining 2 tablespoons olive oil and add to the bulgur along with the salt and cilantro. Mix well and serve.

Serves 6 to 8

Makluba - Upside Down Rice

Makluba, which means "upside down" in Arabic, is a traditional Arab dish that is cooked in layers in a big pot, then flipped upside down just before serving. Traditional recipes typically include chicken, which I don't eat, so this is my vegetarian version.

¼ cauliflower, cut into florets

1 medium eggplant, cut into slices or 2x2-cm cubes

2 zucchini, thickly sliced

Olive oil

Salt

1-2 medium potatoes, thickly sliced

2 cups basmati or Jasmine rice

½ tsp. cinnamon

½ tsp. ground allspice

½ tsp. ground cardamom

1 tsp. ground coriander

1-2 tsp. turmeric

1 tsp. salt

4 cups water or vegetable broth

Chopped parsley

Almond slivers or pine nuts, toasted

1. Preheat the oven to 250°C/480°F.

2. Put the cauliflower, eggplant and zucchini in separate baking pan and toss with olive oil and salt. Bake for 20 minutes, until golden brown. Remove from the oven and set aside.

3. Coat the bottom of a large, wide pot with olive oil and place the potato slices in an even layer.

4. Spread half of the vegetables on top. Pour half of the rice over to cover and arrange the remaining vegetables on top. Finish with the rice.

5. Mix the spices with the water or vegetable broth and pour over the rice and vegetables.

6. Put the pot over high heat and bring to a boil. Lower the heat and cook, covered, until the rice is tender and the liquid has absorbed.

7. When ready, remove the lid and place a large serving platter upside down on top of the pot. Carefully flip upside down, banging the bottom of the pot with a spoon to free any stuck bits. Carefully remove the pot.

8. Garnish with parsley and almonds or pine nuts and serve.

Serves 6 to 8

Tabouleh

*A quintessentially Middle Eastern grain salad, tabouleh is light, fresh and colorful.
Pomegranates and radish are not typical additions, but when they're in season they
beautifully complement the other ingredients and make the salad pop visually.
I learned to season my tabouleh with cinnamon and allspice from an Arab friend.*

½ cup fine bulgur

½ cup hot water

½ cup lemon juice, plus more to taste

4-5 spring onions, sliced

2-3 tomatoes, finely diced

1 cucumber, finely diced

3 cups finely chopped flat-leaf parsley

½ cup finely chopped mint

5 Tbs. olive oil

Salt & pepper

Za'atar, sumac, or cinnamon and allspice

Pomegranate seeds (optional)

1. Soak the bulgur in hot water and lemon juice for about 20 minutes. Drain and put in a serving bowl.

2. Add the spring onions, tomatoes, cucumber, parsley, mint, olive oil and lemon juice to taste, salt and pepper. Sprinkle with za'atar or sumac, or a mixture of cinnamon and allspice.

3. Taste for seasoning and add more olive oil or lemon juice if needed. If it's too dry add more lemon juice. Toss well, cover and let sit for an hour or two at room temperature (don't refrigerate as the freshness of the herbs will be lost).

Varitions:

- Substitute the bulgur with couscous.

- For gluten free tabouleh, use shredded cauliflower instead of bulgur.

TIP: Add some finely diced radishes for a crunchy texture.

Serves 4 to 6

Bukharan Chickpea Pastry

There's a similar Iraqi pastry called sambusak that is made with a different pastry,
filled and fried. This Bukharan version gives you a similar dish without the frying.
It's easy and simple and, unlike sambusak, you don't have to individually fill or
fry pastries, which can be tedious and time consuming.

1 onion, chopped

Olive oil

2 tsp. black mustard seeds

2 tsp. cumin

1 tsp. salt

1 tsp. turmeric

2 cups cooked or canned chickpeas, mashed

1 (30x60-cm) sheet puff pastry

1 egg, lightly beaten

Sesame or nigella (black cumin) seeds

1. Fry the onion in a pan with the olive oil and spices until caramelized.

2. Remove from the heat. Add to the mashed chickpeas and mix well.

3. Preheat the oven to 200°C/400°F.

4. Unroll the dough and divide in half.

5. Spread the chickpea and onion mixture evenly over both pastry halves. Roll each lengthwise into a log and transfer to a parchment paper-lined baking sheet.

6. Brush the tops of the dough with the egg and sprinkle with sesame or nigella seeds.

7. Bake for about 20 minutes, until golden brown and crispy.

8. Remove from the oven and cut into slices.

9. Serve with fresh tomato sauce, tahini sauce (page 126), pickles and hard-boiled egg.

Varition:

- Use phyllo dough instead of puff pastry. Use a number of sheets, brushing a little melted butter or olive oil between each layer before filling and rolling it with the chickpea mixture.

Makes 2 loaves

Falafel

Over the years, falafel has become one of the official foods of Israel. I started making it because I always have requests for it in my cooking classes. Especially with homemade pita and zhug, this is even better than what you'll find at most falafel stands.

1 cup dried chickpeas

¼ bunch parsley

¼ bunch cilantro

1 small onion

2-3 cloves garlic

1-2 tsp. salt

1 tsp. paprika

2 tsp. cumin

2 tsp. ground coriander

¼ tsp. baking soda or powder

Vegetable oil for frying

1. Put the chickpeas in a large bowl and cover with water. Allow to soak overnight.

2. Drain the water and rinse the chickpeas.

3. Grind the chickpeas with the parsley, cilantro, onion and garlic in a meat grinder or food processor. Process until blended but not pureed.

4. Mix in the salt, paprika, cumin and coriander.

5. Knead the mixture, cover and refrigerate for at least 30 minutes.

6. Heat a few inches of oil in a deep, heavy-bottomed pot.

7. Remove falafel mixture from the fridge and mix in the baking soda or powder. If the mixture is dry, mix in 2 to 3 tablespoons water.

8. Using spoons or a falafel scoop, form into small balls.

9. Fry 1 ball in the hot oil to test the texture and taste. Adjust the seasoning as necessary.

10. Working in batches, fry the remaining falafel balls for a few minutes per side, until golden brown. Transfer to a mesh sieve.

11. Serve on their own or in a pita (page 130) with tahini sauce (page 126), cabbage salad (page 50) and zhug (page 98).

TIPs: 1. *Putting fried foods like falafel and latkes in a mesh sieve instead of on paper towels helps keep them nice and crispy.*

2. *How do you know that the oil is hot enough for deep frying? When you insert a wooden stick you should see bubbles (see picture).*

Makes about 20 falafel balls

Hummus

This recipe is the superstar of any culinary tour in Israel. Although you can use canned chickpeas, if you want to make authentic hummus you must start with dry chickpeas. It takes a little bit of forethought but not that much more work and it's worth it.

2 cups dried chickpeas

1 medium onion, peeled and cut into quarters

5 cloves garlic

1 bunch fresh parsley (optional)

1 tsp. cumin (optional)

4-5 Tbs. tahini

Juice of 1 lemon

Salt

olive oil

Paprika

Coarsely chopped parsley leaves

1. Put the chickpeas in a large bowl, cover with water and soak overnight. Change the soaking water at least once.

2. Drain and rinse the chickpeas, put in a large pot and cover with plenty of cold water. Add the onion and garlic and bring to a boil. Simmer until the chickpeas are tender, 2 to 3 hours. (Alternately, cook in a pressure cooker for at least 1½ hours after it starts to boil.) Add the parsley and cumin to the cooking water if you like.

3. Drain the chickpeas and remove the herbs, reserving some of the cooking liquid.

4. Set aside ¼ cup of the chickpeas. Grind the remaining chickpeas along with the cooked onion and garlic in food processor or hand blender.

5. Gradually add tahini, lemon juice and salt until you have a smooth, uniform paste. Slowly pour in reserved chickpea liquid until the desired consistency is reached.

6. Taste and adjust seasoning.

7. Pour into a bowl and serve topped with a drizzle of olive oil, the reserved chickpeas, paprika and coarsely chopped parsley leaves.

Varition:

- Make green hummus by adding ½ bunch fresh parsley and ½ bunch fresh cilantro.

TIP: You can freeze the cooked chickpeas and cooking water separately in small quantities and defrost before making your hummus.

Serves 6

Fuul

This Egyptian dip made from dried (not fresh!) fava beans has become an Israeli classic. Fuul (which rhymes with pool) is often served as a topping or side along with hummus and always comes with hard boiled eggs and pita bread. The buttermilk in the tahini sauce makes it luscious and just a little tangy.

Fuul

1-2 cups dried fava beans

4-5 cloves garlic (optional)

Cumin

Paprika

Chopped parsley

Hard boiled egg

Pita bread

1. Soak the fava beans overnight and change the soaking water at least once. Drain.

2. Put the soaked fava beans and garlic in a large pot and cover with cold water. Boil, covered, for about 20 minutes, then lower the heat and cook until softened, about 2 hours. Add additional boiling water if necessary.

3. Drain the fava beans and mash with a fork.

4. Drizzle with tahini sauce and garnish with cumin, paprika and parsley. Serve with a hard-boiled egg and fresh pita bread.

Tahini Sauce

½ cup tahini

½ cup buttermilk or drinking yogurt

Juice of 1 lemon

1. Whisk together the tahini and buttermilk until very smooth and thick.

2. Slowly whisk in the lemon juice until you reach the desired flavor and consistency - it should be very smooth and just thin enough to drizzle.

Variation:

- It is nice also to mash together fava beans with cooked chickpeas.

Serves 6

Breads

are my love and my weakness. I never say no to fresh bread and nothing can compare to the smell of it baking in the oven. A number of years ago I stopped buying bread and haven't looked back. I've chosen here recipes that even the novice baker can easily make and feel like a pro.

Pita | Challah | Beer Bread | Home Bread | No Knead Bread | Rolls with Sunflower Seeds

Pita

Making your own pita bread may seem intimidating, but it's not nearly as hard as it looks. And once you've made your own, it's hard to go back to store-bought versions.

500 g (3½ cups) all-purpose flour

1 tsp. salt

15 g (4 tsp.) fresh yeast or 8 g (2 tsp.) dry yeast

1 Tbs. brown sugar

1½ Tbs. olive oil

350 g (1½ cups) water

1. Put a large baking sheet in the oven and preheat to 220°C/450°F.

2. Put the flour in the bowl of a stand mixer and mix with the salt.

3. Sprinkle the yeast and sugar over (the yeast shouldn't directly touch any salt).

4. Add the olive oil and half of the water and begin mixing with the dough hook.

5. Gradually add the remaining water while mixing. The dough should look sticky.

6. Knead the dough for about 10 minutes, until it is soft and separates from the sides of the bowl.

7. Cover and let rise for about 1 hour, until doubled in volume.

8. Turn out the dough onto a lightly floured surface and create 8 to 10 even balls of dough. Cover and let rise in a warm place for another 10 minutes.

9. Flatten each ball to discs of about 8 cm. in diameter.

10. Bake on the hot baking sheet for 10 minutes. The pita is ready when it puffs up slightly from the air in the middle.

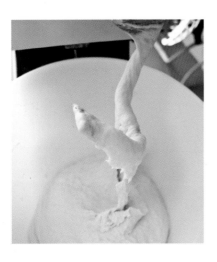

Makes 8 to 10 pitas

Challah

One of the most important Jewish foods, challah is eaten on Shabbat and holidays. I've always loved the smell of fresh baked bread at home, but before I started making my own I thought it was very complicated and difficult. Then I started trying lots of recipes and have come up with this one, which produces a satisfying challah every time. Now that I make my own bread often, I think it's easy.

320 g (10 oz) water

80 g (2.7 oz) sugar

30 g (3 Tbs.) fresh yeast or 15 g (1½ Tbs.) dry yeast

800 g (25½ oz) all-purpose flour

2 eggs

12 g (1 Tbs.) salt

60 g (2 oz) oil

For the coating:

1 egg, lightly beaten

2-3 Tbs. sesame/poppy/sunflower seeds

1. Pour the water, sugar and yeast into the bowl of a stand mixer fitted with a dough hook.

2. Add the flour, eggs, salt and oil.

3. Mix on low for 4 minutes. Increase the speed and mix for another 5 minutes.

4. Take the dough from the bowl and put it on a floured surface. Knead with your hands a few times and roll it into a ball. Don't worry if the dough looks a little moist; do not be tempted to add more flour!

5. Place the dough in a lightly floured bowl and cover with a kitchen towel. Allow to rise for about 40 minutes, until doubled in volume.

6. Divide the dough in half. Divide each half into three portions and roll them into a thick snake. Pinch together the tops of three pieces of dough and braid, pinching at the end. Repeat with the remaining dough to make two loaves.

Makes 2 loaves challah

7. Place on a parchment-lined baking sheet.

8. Allow the dough to rise once more on the baking sheet. Check with your finger to see if it's ready: push the dough gently with your finger; if it bounces back quickly, then it's ready to bake.

9. Brush with egg and sprinkle with sesame, poppy or sunflower seeds.

10. Meanwhile, preheat the oven to 200°C/400°F.

11. Put the challah in the oven. Bake for 10 minutes, then lower the heat to 170°C/340°F. Bake for 10 minutes, until golden brown.

12. Remove from the oven and allow to cool slightly before serving.

Variation:

*   Instead of braiding the challah dough, divide it into 19 even pieces and roll them into balls. Arrange them next to each other in a tight circle to form 3 round challah loaves. Brush with egg and bake as directed above.

TIP: When making challah, babka and other recipes with yeast dough, press lightly on the dough with your finger until it makes a slight dent. If the dent vanishes immediately it's a sign that the dough has risen and is ready to the next step of baking. If the dent remains unchanged, then the dough hasn't risen sufficiently.

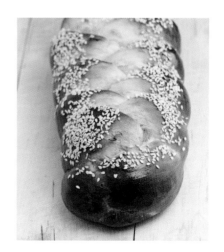

Beer Bread

If you are intimidated by making bread at home, then this recipe is a perfect introduction. There's no kneading, very little rising and beer is used instead of traditional baking yeast, which can be fickle.

165 g (5½ oz) all purpose flour

165 g (5½ oz) whole wheat flour

10 g (1 Tbs.) baking powder

330 ml (11 oz) beer

½ tsp. salt

1. In a large mixing bowl, mix together the flours, baking powder, beer and salt.

2. Transfer to a parchment-lined loaf pan and leave to rest for 1 hour.

3. Meanwhile, preheat the oven to 170°C/340°F.

4. Bake for 50 minutes, until evenly browned.

5. Remove from the pan and cool on a wire rack.

Variations:

- Add ½ cup grated cheese (like Parmesan) to the dough.

- Add chopped olives to the dough.

- Make the bread sweet with chopped dried dates and figs.

- Toss in chopped walnuts to the dough.

Makes 1 loaf

Home Bread

This healthy bread is filled with whole wheat flour, oats, flax seeds and walnuts. It's especially easy to make since you start it in a cold oven, so there's no need to worry about preheating. This would make a great sandwich bread and is even good the next day.

2 cups warm water

1 Tbs. brown sugar

1½ Tbs. dry yeast

2 cups all-purpose flour

2 cups whole wheat flour

1 cup rolled oats

3 Tbs. flax seeds

2 tsp. salt

Handful walnuts (optional)

1. Mix together the water, sugar and yeast in the bowl of a stand mixer.

2. Add the flours, oats, flax seeds, salt and walnuts (if using) and knead in a stand mixer fitted with a dough hook for 7 minutes, until the dough separates from the side of the bowl. If it's too moist add another 1 to 2 tablespoons of flour.

3. Transfer the dough to a greased or parchment – lined loaf pan, cover with a kitchen towel and allow to rise until doubled in volume.

4. Put in a cold oven and set the temperature to 200°C/400°F. Bake for 35 minutes, until golden brown.

5. Remove from the oven and immediately turn out onto a cooling rack (this prevents it from sweating in the pan). Allow to cool before slicing.

Makes 1 loaf

No Knead Bread

This bread takes a little bit of forethought since it needs to rise overnight, but other than that it requires very little work. And the result will be a gorgeous, crusty loaf of bread that looks as though it came straight from the bakery!

½ tsp. dry yeast

350 g (1½ cups) warm water

220 g (1½ cups) white flour

200 g (1½ cups) whole wheat flour

1½ tsp. salt

1. Put all the ingredients in a bowl and mix with a spoon until fully combined and slightly sticky.

2. Cover the bowl with plastic wrap and leave to rise at room temperature for 12 hours (overnight). You should start to see lots of bubbles.

3. Dust a wooden board with flour.

4. Turn out the dough onto the board and fold over a few times. Cover with a dish towel and leave to rise for another 2 hours.

5. Put a Dutch oven in the oven and preheat to 250°C/480°F.

6. Once it is hot, sprinkle the Dutch oven with flour and put the dough inside.

7. Cover and bake for 30 minutes. Remove the lid, reduce the temperature to 180°C/350°F and bake for another 20 minutes, until the bread is evenly browned.

8. Remove from the oven and transfer the bread to a rack to cool before slicing.

Makes 1 loaf

Rolls with Sunflower Seeds

This was inspired by a recipe someone gave me 30 years ago that I had scribbled on a scrap of paper. The original recipe had onions and garlic, which my kids don't like. Over the years I developed this version, which everyone loves.

240 g (8 oz) water

2 Tbs. dry yeast

2 Tbs. brown sugar

250 g (8 oz) all-purpose flour

200 g (6.4 oz) whole wheat flour

50 g (1½ oz) bran

1 tsp. salt

50 g (1½ oz) butter, cut into small pieces

2 Tbs. sunflower seeds, plus more for topping

1 egg, lightly beaten

1. Put the water, yeast and sugar in a mixing bowl and whisk until the yeast is fully dissolved. Set aside.

2. Mix the flours, bran and salt. Pour it on top of the yeast mixture in the bowl of a stand mixer fitted with a dough hook and mix on low.

3. Add the butter and knead on high for a few minutes, until the dough comes together. Knead for a few more minutes.

4. Add the sunflower seeds and mix for a few minutes.

5. Turn out the dough onto a floured surface and roll into a long, thick snake.

6. Cut into 12 equal pieces. Knead each piece a little between your palm and fingers and roll into a ball.

7. Put on a lined baking sheet, cover with a dish towel and let rise until doubled in size (time will vary depending on the temperature of your house, but about 1 hour).

8. Meanwhile, preheat the oven to 190°C/375°F.

9. Brush the rolls with egg and sprinkle with more sunflower seeds.

10. Bake for 15 minutes, rotating the pan halfway through, until golden brown.

11. Remove from the oven and allow to cool just slightly before serving.

Variation:

- Replace the butter with an equal amount of olive oil for healthier (and parve) rolls.

Makes 12 rolls

Although I am a vegetarian, I do eat **Fish**. *Living right on the Mediterranean, fresh fish is plentiful and so good for you. It's also traditional for many holidays. For instance we serve whole fish with its head on for Rosh Hashanah (Jewish New Year) to symbolize that we should be the head and not the tail.*

Sephardic Style Baked Fish with Vegetables | Fish in Tomato Sauce Jewish-Turkish Style | Moroccan Style Fish with Couscous | Chraime | Fish with Green Tahini Sauce Fish Siniye | Fish Kebabs with Yellow Tahini Yogurt Sauce | Fish Balls with Chickpeas and Swiss Chard

Sephardic Style Baked Fish with Vegetables

Sephardic cooking uses lots of tomato paste, onion, garlic and herbs, as evidenced by this recipe. This recipe also includes turmeric, which is also used in some parts of the Sephardic cuisine. Besides having a wonderful flavor, turmeric also boasts lots of health properties.

1 whole fish (1-2 lbs) or cut into pieces (grouper, mullet, red drum, tilapia)

Olive oil

2 onions, sliced

4-5 garlic cloves, sliced

1 red hot pepper, sliced and seeds removed

3 tomatoes, roughly chopped

1 Tbs. tomato paste diluted with ¼ cup water

½ bunch parsley, chopped

2 tsp. salt

Juice from 2 lemons

1 cup water

1 tsp. cumin

1 tsp. turmeric

Pine nuts, toasted

1. Heat the oven to 180°C/350°F.

2. Place fish in a baking pan.

3. Fry onions in olive oil until transparent.

4. Add the garlic, pepper, tomatoes, diluted tomato paste, parsley and salt. Cook for a few more minutes.

5. Pour the sauce on top of the fish.

6. Mix lemon juice with the water, cumin and turmeric and pour over the fish. Add more water if necessary to cover the fish ¾ with liquid.

7. Bake for approximately 30 minutes, periodically ladling sauce over the fish to prevent it from drying out.

8. Sprinkle with toasted pine nuts before serving.

Serves 6

Fish in Tomato Sauce Jewish-Turkish Style

This dish reminds me of my childhood flavors as my mother included tomato sauce in many dishes. It tastes so good. Be sure to have plenty of bread on hand to sop up any leftover sauce.

Olive oil

1 onion, chopped

1-2 Tbs. tomato paste

1-2 cloves garlic, sliced

3-4 tomatoes, diced

Chopped cilantro or parsley

1 hot pepper, sliced (optional)

1 tsp. sugar (optional)

Salt & pepper

6 fish filets (grouper, mullet, red drum or tilapia all work well)

1. Preheat the oven to 190°C/375°F.

2. Fry the chopped onions in olive oil until softened.

3. Add the tomato paste, garlic, tomatoes, cilantro or parsley, hot pepper, sugar (if using), salt and pepper and a bit of water. Cook until the tomatoes soften. Keep warm.

4. Place the fish in a large baking pan and pour the sauce over.

5. Bake for about 10 minutes, until the fish is cooked through and the sauce dense.

6. Garnish with additional fresh cilantro or parsley before serving.

Variation:

• Fry the fish in a nonstick pan for 2 minutes per side, until cooked through. Transfer the fish to plates and spoon the sauce over.

Moroccan Style Fish with Couscous

This fish cooked with vegetables is at once homey and elegant and the couscous perfectly soaks up the lovely sauce. Although you can use store-bought instant couscous, this shortcut version makes preparing your own couscous from scratch a cinch.

Moroccan Style Fish

5 cloves garlic, halved

1-2 hot green peppers (optional)

2 carrots, sliced

1-2 potatoes, thickly sliced

2 Tbs. sweet paprika

½ Tbs. hot paprika (optional)

1 tsp. cumin

1 tsp. ground coriander

1 tsp. salt

2 Tbs. olive oil

1 Tbs. tomato paste

6 fish filets
(tilapia, grouper, or mullet all work well)

½ bunch cilantro, roughly chopped

1. Put the garlic, hot peppers, carrots and potatoes in the bottom of a wide-rimmed sauté pan and cover with water. Cook over medium heat until the vegetables are soft.

2. In a small bowl, mix together the sweet and hot paprika, cumin, coriander, salt, olive oil and tomato paste. Add to the pot and cook for another 5 minutes.

3. Place the fish on top of the vegetables, ladle some sauce over, cover and cook for about 10 minutes. Don't uncover or stir, but gently shake the pot every few minutes to mix the sauce.

4. Garnish with chopped cilantro and serve with the couscous.

Couscous

2 cups water

¼ cup olive or canola oil

½ Tbs. salt

2 cups fine semolina

1. Put the water, oil and salt in a pot and bring to a boil.

2. Pour over the semolina, stirring constantly until all the water is absorbed.

3. Cover and cook for 7 minutes over very low heat.

4. Break up the semolina with a fork into little crumbs or push through a sieve.

TIP: Instead of breaking up the semolina with a fork, put it in the refrigerator until it is very cold, then pulse in a food processor.

Serves 6

Chraime - Moroccan-Style Fish in Spicy Red Sauce

Chraime is a traditional North African dish made of fish and piquant red sauce. It's particularly popular in the Jewish communities of Morocco, Libya and Tunisia.

1½ Tbs. sweet Moroccan paprika*

½-1 Tbs. hot paprika

2 cloves garlic, chopped

1 Tbs. salt

1¼ cup water

¼-½ cup olive oil

2 Tbs. tomato paste

½ Tbs. cumin

½ Tbs. ground caraway

6 fish slices
(such as grouper, mullet, or red drum)

Juice of 1 lemon

1. In a small bowl, mix the sweet and hot paprika, garlic, salt and ½ cup of the water.

2. Heat olive oil in a large pan and add the spice mixture. Stir and cook for a few minutes.

3. Add the tomato paste and another ½ cup water and cook for another few minutes.

4. Add the cumin, caraway and fish. Pour the lemon juice on top of the fish and simmer, uncovered, until the fish is almost cooked through.

5. Add the remaining ¼ cup water if needed and cook for another 10 minutes, until the sauce thickens.

6. Serve hot with fresh bread or on top of couscous.

* Moroccan paprika is made with oil while regular paprika is dry.

TIP: For added flavor, cook the fish head in the sauce.

Serves 6

Fish with Green Tahini Sauce

This is my interpretation of traditional Arabic siniye. The tahini sauce complements the fish nicely and is very easy to prepare - it can be made with any white fish.

Olive oil

2 tomatoes, sliced

4 tilapia filets (or any white fish)

½ cup boiled or canned chickpeas (optional)

½ cup tahini

½ cup finely chopped parsley

½ cup finely chopped cilantro

1-2 cloves garlic, chopped

Juice of 1 lemon, plus more to taste

1 cup water

½ tsp. salt

1. Preheat the oven to 190°C/375°F.

2. Pour olive oil in a thin, even layer to coat the bottom of a baking dish.

3. Arrange slices of tomato along the bottom of the baking dish and top with the fish filets. Spread the chickpeas on top, if using.

4. Using a hand blender or food processor, mix the tahini, parsley, cilantro, garlic, lemon juice, water and salt until it is a smooth, green, diluted sauce.

5. Pour the tahini sauce over the fish and bake for about 20 minutes, until the sauce thickens.

6. Remove from the heat and serve.

Variation:

- To make fish with red tahini sauce, mix together 1 chopped tomato with the tahini, parsley, garlic, lemon juice and salt as directed above (omit the cilantro). Leave out the tomato slices and chickpeas from the recipe above, pour the red tahini sauce over the fish and continue as directed.

Serves 4

Siniye - Fish in Tahini Sauce

Baking vegetables, meat and fish in tahini (see also my eggplant siniye recip, page 30) is an Arab technique that I've picked up and adapted. Since I don't eat red meat, I prefer this lighter version with fish.

6 fish filets or slices
(such as grouper, mullet, or tilapia)

Flour

¼ cup olive oil

1 onion, chopped

5 cloves garlic, minced

2 tomatoes, diced

Chopped parsley

½ tsp. salt

Pepper

½ cup tahini

1 cup water

Juice of 1 lemon

Pine nuts

1. Preheat the oven to 190°C/375°F.

2. Lightly coat the fish in flour.

3. Heat the olive oil over medium heat in an ovenproof skillet. Add the fish and fry for 2 minutes per side. Transfer the fish to a plate and set aside.

4. Add the onion and garlic to the pan and fry for 2 to 3 minutes.

5. Add the tomatoes, a handful of chopped parsley, salt and pepper. Cook until the tomatoes have softened.

6. Mix the tahini with the water and lemon juice to create a diluted sauce.

7. Put the fish back in the pan and pour the tahini sauce over. Sprinkle with pine nuts.

8. Bake for about 10 minutes, until the tahini sauce is dense.

9. Remove from the oven and garnish with additional chopped parsley before serving.

Serves 6

Fish Kebabs with Yellow Tahini Yogurt Sauce

Packed with fresh herbs, these fish kebabs are bursting with flavor. Since there are no binding ingredients like eggs, the secret is to knead the mixture like dough to break down the proteins. The kebabs are good on their own, but even better with the creamy yellow tahini sauce.

Fish Kebabs

1 kg (2.2 lb) fish filet, finely chopped
(such as tilapia, sea bass, mullet or red drum)

2 shallots or 1 small red onion, finely chopped

½ bunch parsley leaves, finely chopped

½ bunch mint leaves, finely chopped

½ bunch cilantro leaves, finely chopped

Lemon zest

2 cloves garlic, minced

6 tablespoons olive oil

Salt & pepper

1. Mix together all the kebab ingredients in a large bowl and knead until you obtain a uniform mixture.

2. Cover and refrigerate for 30 minutes.

3. Shape into small round or oblong patties. Working in batches, cook on a hot grill or skillet for 3 to 4 minutes per side until cooked through and golden.

4. Transfer to a plate or put in a pita and serve with a generous spoonful of the tahini yogurt sauce.

Yellow Tahini Yogurt Sauce

2 tablespoons oil

½ tablespoon ground turmeric

½ cup tahini paste

1 cup thick goat's milk yogurt or buttermilk (preferably drinking yogurt)

Juice of ½ lemon, or more to taste

1 clove garlic, minced

Salt

1. Heat the oil and turmeric in a pan until just before boiling, or heat for 30 seconds in microwave. Strain and allow to cool fully before proceeding.

2. Mix together the turmeric oil with the remaining sauce ingredients until smooth and pale yellow in color.

Fish Balls with Chickpeas and Swiss Chard

These fish balls are a great alternative for those like me who don't eat meat. I love the bright, bold flavor of this sauce that just explodes in your mouth.

For the Fish Balls:

½ kg. (1 lb) fish filet, minced
(tilapia, sea bass, mullet or red drum)

1 small red onion, finely chopped

½ bunch parsley leaves, finely chopped

½ bunch mint leaves, finely chopped

½ bunch cilantro leaves, finely chopped

Zest of 1 lemon

2 cloves garlic, minced

Salt & pepper

1 egg, lightly beaten

⅓ cup breadcrumbs

Chili flakes (optional)

For the Stewed Swiss Chard and Chickpeas:

5 Tbs. olive oil, plus more as needed

1 onion, chopped

3-4 cloves garlic, sliced

1-2 carrots, sliced

1 celeriac, peeled and diced

1 bunch Swiss chard, roughly chopped (leaves and stalks separated)

1 cup cooked chickpeas

1 cup white wine (optional)

Juice of 2 lemons

1. Make the fish balls: Mix together all the ingredients for the fish balls and knead well until you obtain a uniform mixture. Leave to rest in the fridge for at least 30 minutes.

2. Make the sauce: Heat 3 tablespoons of the olive oil in a large, deep sauté pan and add the onion, garlic, carrots, celeriac and Swiss chard stalks. Cover and simmer over low heat for about 10 minutes, until the vegetables are tender.

3. Add the chickpeas with some of their cooking liquid, wine and the juice of 1 lemon. Increase the heat to high and cook, uncovered, for 2 to 3 minutes.

4. Remove the fish mixture from the fridge and form into small balls. Carefully drop in the sauce with part of the Swiss chard leaves.

5. Spoon the sauce over the fish balls so they are almost completely covered and cook, uncovered, for about 10 minutes.

6. Taste and improve the seasoning. Add the remaining Swiss chard leaves, juice of the remaining lemon and the remaining 2 tablespoons olive oil.

7. Serve with rice, couscous, or bread.

Serves 6

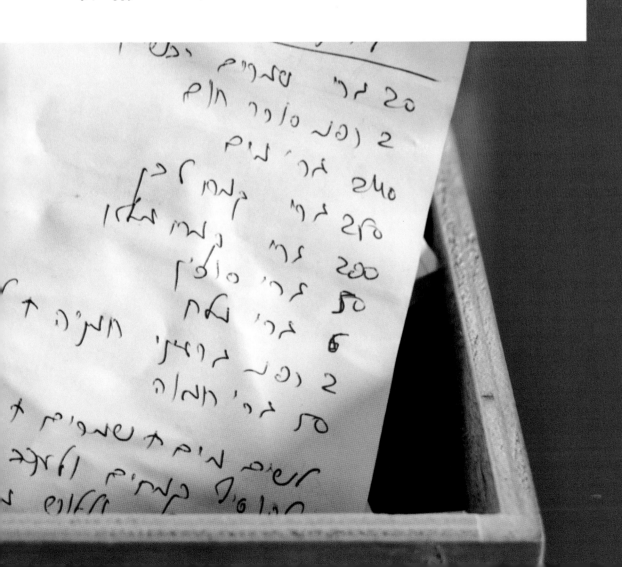

Family Recipes

Although I make all the recipes in this book often, the dishes in this section are particularly close to my heart. These are the dishes that my family requests again and again, the comfort food of my children and recipes passed down by my mother and grandmother. This is my personal cuisine.

Sfongato - Eggplant Pie | Baked Pasta | Borekas | Borekitas | Olive and Cheese Rolls
Hashwa - Rice with Meat | Meatballs in Tomato Sauce | Salmon Baked with Mustard and
Honey | Poppy Seed Cake | Chocolate Cake

Sfongato - Eggplant Pie

This Greek eggplant pie is my mother's recipe and one I make often at home.
Kashkaval is a cheese found in the Balkans, Turkey and Greece, where my mother is from.
This is one of those dishes that doesn't look all that pretty, but is utterly delicious.

1-2 eggplants

1 Tbs. olive oil

100 g (3½ oz) Bulgarian or feta cheese

100 g (3½ oz) Kashkaval, grated
(substitute caciocavallo or provolone)

1 potato, cooked and mashed

2 eggs

1. Heat the oven to 180°C/350°F.

2. Roast the eggplants until evenly charred. Cut a slit at the bottom of the eggplant and place in a sieve. Leave to drain.

3. Once cool enough to handle, peel the burnt skin, remove the dark seeds and roughly chop.

4. Mix the chopped eggplants with the olive oil, Bulgarian and kashkaval cheeses, mashed potato and eggs until thoroughly combined.

5. Put in a baking pan and bake for 30 to 40 minutes, until lightly browned on the top. Remove from the oven and allow to cool for a few minutes before serving.

Variation:

- Use boiled, chopped leeks instead of eggplant.

Serves 4 to 6

Baked Pasta

This dish, which is something my mother used to make, is now a favorite of my children. It's great because you can use whatever bits of cheese you have on hand and is also a good use for leftover pasta. Because it's full of cheese, this baked pasta is also perfect for the holiday of Shavuot.

500 g (1 lb) pasta (I prefer penne)

250 g (8 oz) cottage cheese

200 g (7 oz) sour cream or cream cheese

150 g (5 oz) feta

150 g (5 oz) reduced fat shredded cheese, such as cheddar

2 Tbs. olive oil

3 large eggs

1. Preheat oven to 180°C/350°F.

2. Cook the pasta according to package directions, until al dente. Drain and set aside.

3. In a large bowl, thoroughly mix together the cheeses. Mix in the olive oil and eggs, then the pasta.

4. Put in a large baking dish and bake for about 30 minutes, turning the dish halfway through, until bubbly and lightly browned on top.

5. Remove from the oven and allow to cool for a few minutes before serving.

Variations:

- Mix in some ketchup to the cheese mixture (this is how my daughter prefers it).

- Add in thyme, oregano, or whatever fresh or dried herbs you feel like.

- Grate Parmesan on top if you like.

TIP: Use a glass baking dish so you can keep an eye on the bottom and make sure it doesn't burn.

Serves 6 to 8

Borekas

Borekas are a Balkan, cheese-stuffed pastry. My parents were both from Greece so this was always our Shabbat breakfast. In Israel borekas are widely available both fresh and frozen, with a variety of fillings.

200 g (7 oz) feta or Bulgarian cheese

250 g (8 oz) quark or ricotta

¼ cup grated Cheddar or Pecorino

1 egg

1 Tbs. corn starch (if mixture is too wet)

1 sheet puff pastry dough, defrosted

For the Topping:

1 egg, lightly beaten

Sesame or nigella seeds

1. Preheat the oven to 180°C/350°F.

2. Mix together all the cheeses with the egg. Add the corn starch if the mixture is very wet.

3. Roll out the puff pastry just a little and cut it into even squares.

4. Put a teaspoon of filling in the center of each square, brush the edges with egg and fold into a triangle. Pinch at the tip to seal.

5. Transfer the borekas to a parchment-lined baking sheet. Brush with egg and sprinkle with sesame or nigella seeds.

6. Bake for 20 to 30 minutes, until golden brown.

7. Remove from the oven, cool and serve.

Makes 16 to 18

Borekitas

These small borekas are Sephardic-Greek style and yet another recipe that I learned to make from my mother. There's cheese both in the dough and the filling, making them a great source of calcium and an excellent snack for kids.

For the Dough:

2 cups self-rising flour

⅓ cup canola oil

250 g (8 oz) soft white cheese or cream cheese

1 tsp. salt

For the Filling:

1 small mashed potato
(if using soft white cheese)

150 g (5 oz) feta

250 g (8 oz) soft white cheese or cream cheese

1 egg

For the Topping:

1 egg, lightly beaten

Sesame seeds

1. Mix together the dough ingredients and refrigerate for 1 hour.

2. Preheat the oven to 180°C/350°F.

3. Mix all the filling ingredients together until smooth.

4. Divide the dough in four portions and roll each into thin sheet.

5. Cut out 20 or so circles from the dough using a cup or cookie cutter.

6. Put 1 teaspoon of filling in the center of each circle, fold in half to form a semi-circle and pinch down to seal.

7. Brush the top of the dough with egg and sprinkle with sesame seeds.

8. Transfer to a parchment paper-lined baking sheet and bake until golden.

9. Remove from the oven, cool and serve.

Makes about 20

Olive and Cheese Rolls

My mother used to make this with butter or margarine, but I started using oil to make it healthier. These rolls are perfect to serve at a party along with cocktails.

For the Dough

2½ cups self-rising flour

150 ml (5 oz) olive oil

150 ml (5 oz) yogurt or sour cream

1 cup grated cheese

For the Filling

250 g (1 cup) soft white cheese or cream cheese

1 egg

Diced olives

Flour or cornstarch

1. Mix together all the dough ingredients until smooth and leave to rest for 30 minutes.

2. Mix together the soft white cheese, egg and diced olives. If the mixture is very runny add 1 to 2 teaspoons flour or cornstarch to thicken. (If using cream cheese it will be thick enough.)

3. Preheat the oven to 180°C/175°F.

4. Divide the dough into half and roll each portion into a thin sheet. Spread the filling evenly across the dough and roll up lengthwise into a tight log. Press down slightly to seal.

5. Using a sharp knife, cut into 1½-cm slices and put on a parchment paper-lined baking sheet.

6. Bake for about 10 minutes, until golden brown.

7. Remove from the oven, cool and serve.

Makes about 20

Meatballs in Tomato Sauce

This is one of my son's favorite dishes. Although similar to Italian-style meatballs, the spices and fresh herbs are characteristic of Sephardic and Mizrahi cooking.

For the meatballs:

½ kg (1 lb) ground beef

1 onion, finely chopped

½ bunch of parsley leaves, finely chopped

1 egg

2-3 Tbs. breadcrumbs

1 tsp. ras-el-hanout or baharat

Salt and pepper

For the sauce:

¼ cup olive oil

1 small onion, chopped

3-4 cloves garlic, chopped

½ Tbs. turmeric

1 Tbs. sweet Moroccan paprika

1 tsp. hot paprika (optional)

1 (400 g/ 14 oz) can crushed tomatoes

Salt

1. Mix together all the meatball ingredients and knead well until you obtain a uniform mixture.

2. Leave the mixture to rest at least 30 minutes in the fridge.

3. Meanwhile, prepare the sauce. Put the olive oil in a large, deep pan with a lid and sauté the onion and garlic with the turmeric and paprika.

4. Add the tomatoes and cook for few minutes.

5. Form the meatballs and carefully put in the sauce.

6. Cook, covered, for about 20 minutes, until cooked through.

7. Taste and season with salt.

8. Serve with couscous, rice or bread.

Serves 6

Salmon Baked with Mustard and Honey

I learned the recipe for the sauce from my aunt a long time ago and I've been making salmon this way for years. It's one of the things that all three of my children love, so I can't touch it. I make a big salmon filet like this every holiday and there are never leftovers.

3 Tbs. mustard

3 Tbs. honey

1 kg. salmon filet (5-6 portions)

1. In a small bowl, mix together the mustard and honey until it forms a smooth, thick sauce.

2. Put the fish in a baking pan and spread the sauce on top. Leave to rest for at least 1 hour before baking.

3. Preheat the oven to 200°C/400°F.

4. Cover the fish with aluminum foil and bake for 20 to 25 minutes, until cooked through.

5. Remove from the oven and serve with rice with turmeric and cinnamon (p. 110) and green beans in tomato sauce (p. 80).

Serves 6

Poppy Seed Cake

Poppy seed cakes are my husband's favorite and I've been making this one since we got married. Now it's a family favorite and is one I make often.

1 cup ground poppy seeds

½ cup sweet wine or warm milk

5 eggs, yolks and whites separated

1¼ cup sugar

2 Tbs. brandy

1 Tbs. lemon zest (optional)

Pinch of salt

½ cup vegetable oil

1½ cups all-purpose flour

1 tsp. baking powder

1. Preheat the oven to 170°C/325°F.

2. Put the poppy seeds in a bowl and pour the warm milk or wine over. Let sit for 10 minutes.

3. In a separate bowl, mix together the egg yolks, ¾ cup of the sugar, brandy, lemon zest (if using), salt and oil.

4. Slowly stir in the soaked poppy seeds, flour and baking powder.

5. In another bowl, whisk together the egg whites with the remaining ½ cup sugar until soft peaks form.

6. Gently fold the egg whites into the cake batter.

7. Pour into a greased 26-cm baking pan and bake for 45 to 50 minutes, until a toothpick inserted in the middle comes out dry.

8. Remove from the oven and allow to cool before slicing.

Variation:

- To make a richer cake, slice it horizontally and spread your favorite chocolate cream topping on the top and bottom then sandwich to make a layer cake.

TIP: Make sure to buy freshly ground poppy seeds.

Makes 1 cake

Chocolate Cake

This has been the birthday cake in my family for a long time. My mother used to make it and now I prepare it for every birthday. It's rich, moist and better than any mix from a box. It's super easy to make since you mix everything all at once and kids and adults just love it.

For the Cake:

2 cups self-rising flour

1½ cups sugar

6 Tbs. cocoa powder

2 eggs, lightly beaten

½ cup canola oil

1 cup milk

1 cup boiling water

For the Frosting:

3-4 Tbs. chocolate spread
(or 70 g dark chocolate, melted)

3 Tbs. milk

Sprinkles

1. Preheat the oven to 170°C/340°F.

2. In a large mixing bowl, mix together the flour, sugar, cocoa powder, eggs, canola oil and milk until smooth.

3. Add the boiling water to the batter and stir until smooth and no lumps remain.

4. Pour into a greased 26-cm cake pan. Bake for 30 minutes, until a toothpick inserted in the middle comes out clean.

5. Meanwhile, make the frosting by melting the chocolate spread or the chocolate with the milk on the stovetop or in a microwave. Stir together until smooth and fully incorporated.

6. Remove the cake from the oven and allow to cool slightly before spreading the frosting on top (you can also omit the frosting if you like). Top with colored sprinkles.

Makes 1 cake

Jewish **Holidays** *are all about the food. Each holiday has special dishes that are full of symbolism and tradition and I've shared my family's favorites with you here. We look forward to making these each year and nothing means Hanukkah like levivot and soufganiyot, just as Shavuot wouldn't be the same without cheesecake.*

Leek Patties | Apple Jam | Honey Cake | Hanukkah Levivot | Zucchini Pancakes with Mint Yogurt Sauce | Sweet Cheese Levivot | Soufganiyot | Dried Fruit and Nut Cookies Hamantaschen | Passover Rolls | Passover Brownies | Almond Chocolate Chip Cookies Cheesecake | Semolina Delight

Rosh Hashanah:
Leek Patties

A common dish in Greece, Turkey and Bulgaria, this recipe for leek patties (keftes de prasa) is my mother's. While it is often made with meat, this is a vegetarian version. We typically eat these fried patties at Rosh Hashanah and the entire plate disappears in minutes!

1 kg (2.2 lbs) leeks, trimmed and cleaned

1 egg

Salt

3 Tbs. breadcrumbs

Oil for frying

1. Put cleaned leeks in a pot of water over medium-low heat, cover and cook until soft (they should be tender when poked with a spoon).

2. Drain the leeks and allow to cool. Squeeze out as much liquid as possible.

3. Put the leeks in a food processor and blend until smooth.

4. Mix in the egg, salt and breadcrumbs. The mixture should be quite soft but just firm enough to form into patties.

5. Put about 1 cm oil in a pan over medium heat.

6. Form the leek mixture into small patties and carefully drop in the oil. Fry until evenly browned and crispy on both sides.

7. Transfer to paper towel-lined plate. Serve immediately.

Variation:

• Leek patties are also very popular during Passover. To make them kosher for Passover, simply swap the breadcrumbs for matzo meal.

TIP: To clean leeks, cut in half lengthwise and rinse thoroughly, then soak in a solution of water and a little distilled vinegar. The vinegar will draw the dirt out of the leeks.

Makes about 20

Rosh Hashanah:
Apple Jam

On Rosh Hashanah it is common to eat apples and honey to symbolize a sweet new year. This is my mother's traditional apple jam for the holiday, which we eat every year.

2 kg (4.4 lb) Granny Smith apples

1 kg. (2.2 lb) sugar

20 g vanilla sugar

1½ cups of water

½ cup freshly squeezd lemon juice

1. Peel and grate the apples.

2. Put the grated apples, sugar, vanilla sugar and water in a pot over medium heat. Cook for about 10 minutes, then add the lemon juice.

3. Check consistency of the jam, by pouring a bit of the mixture on a cold plate. The jam should not be too fluid and not too strong. It is ready when it just stays still on the plate.

4. Allow to cool before serving. Store in a tightly sealed glass jar in the fridge for up to a few weeks.

Rosh Hashanah:
Honey Cake

Honey cake is traditionally eaten on Rosh Hashanah, when honey is said to signify a sweet new year. This is my family's favorite and a recipe that I've been making for years. Whereas some honey cakes are dense and heavy, this one uses lots of honey and is light and spongy.

5 eggs, separated into yolks and whites

¾ cup sugar

½ cup vegetable oil

¾ cup honey

1 tsp. cinnamon

¼ tsp. ground cloves

Pinch of salt

1½ cups all-purpose flour

1 tsp. baking powder

1. Preheat the oven to 170°/340°F.

2. In a large bowl, beat together the egg whites and sugar with an electric mixer at high speed until soft peaks form.

3. In a separate bowl, whisk together the egg yolks, oil, honey, cinnamon, cloves and salt.

4. Add the flour to the honey mixture and mix slowly with the mixer on low speed until blended.

5. Gently fold the flour mixture into the egg whites.

6. Pour batter into a large cake pan or 2 loaf pans and bake for 55 to 60 minutes, until golden brown on top and a toothpick inserted in the middle comes out clean. Allow to cool slightly before serving.

TIP: *Use the measuring cup first for the vegetable oil, then the honey. That way the honey will slip right out and won't stick.*

Makes 1 to 2 cakes

Hanukkah:
Hanukkah Levivot

Often called latkes, these Eastern European Jewish potato pancakes are delicious no matter the name. Fried foods are served on Hanukkah since the oil represents the miracle of one night's worth of oil lasting for eight days during the rededication of the Second Temple.

4-5 potatoes, peeled

2 Tbs. flour or potato flour

2 eggs, lightly beaten

1 tsp. salt
(less if you want to eat them with sugar)

Ground pepper
(omit if you want to eat them with sugar)

Oil, for frying

1. Grate the potatoes using the coarse side of a box grater. Put in a colander and squeeze out as much liquid as possible.

2. Put the shredded potato in a bowl and mix with the flour, eggs, salt and pepper.

3. Heat the oil in a wide, heavy-bottomed pan (it should fully coat the bottom of the pan).

4. Add batter by the tablespoonful and fry on both sides until evenly browned and crispy. Transfer to a wire rack while you finish cooking the remaining pancakes.

5. Serve immediately with sour cream or sugar.

Variation:

- Add 1 grated onion, 2 grated carrots, or 1 grated sweet potato to the mixture before frying.

TIP: Keeping the hot pancakes on a wire rack instead of paper towels keeps them nice and crispy.

Serves 6

Hanukkah:
Zucchini Pancakes

These zucchini pancakes are another variation on Hanukkah latkes.
They taste wonderfully fresh, especially if you serve them with minted yogurt.

6 zucchini

2 eggs, lightly beaten

½ cup flour

Salt & pepper

½ cup finely chopped flat-leaf parsley

½ cup finely chopped fresh mint

Canola oil, for frying

1. Grate the zucchini using the coarse side of a box grater. Put in a colander and squeeze out as much liquid as possible.

2. Put the eggs, flour, salt and pepper in a large bowl and mix to combine.

3. Mix in the zucchini, parsley and mint.

4. Heat the canola oil in a wide, heavy-bottomed pan (it should fully coat the bottom of the pan).

5. Form the zucchini mixture into patties and carefully put in the hot oil. Fry on both sides until evenly browned and crispy.

6. Serve with sour cream or yogurt mixed with chopped fresh mint.

TIP: *Put a piece of carrot in the pan while frying to prevent the oil from burning.*

Serves 4 to 6

Hanukkah:
Sweet Cheese 'Levivot'

While the term 'levivot' technically refers to the potato pancakes so common at Hanukkah, this version with sweet cheese is a fun variation that's perfect for dessert. Serve it with sour cream or applesauce, depending on whether you feel like something more sweet or savory.

500g (16 oz) quark or ricotta cheese

150 ml (5 oz) yogurt

⅓ cup sugar

1 tsp. vanilla extract

3 Tbs. raisins (optional)

2 Tbs. brandy

2 eggs

5 Tbs. flour

50 g butter

¼ cup canola oil

Powdered sugar

Sour Cream or applesauce

1. Put the cheese, yogurt, sugar, vanilla extract, raisins (if using), brandy, eggs and flour in a large bowl and mix until smooth.

2. Let the mixture rest in the fridge for 30 minutes.

3. Heat the butter and oil in a wide pan.

4. For each pancake, spoon about ¼ cup of batter into the hot pan. Work in batches so as not to crowd the pan. Fry on both sides until golden and crispy. Transfer to a paper towel-lined plate.

5. Sprinkle with powdered sugar and serve with sour cream or applesauce.

Serves 4 to 6

Hanukkah:
Soufganiyot

Probably the most famous Israeli Hanukkah food, soufganiyot are fried donuts. While they are commonly filled with jelly or other fillings, this recipe makes easy drop donuts. The cheese in the dough gives them a particularly wonderful texture.

1¼ cup self-rising flour

250 g (1 cup) soft white cheese (like ricotta)

2 eggs

2 Tbs. canola oil

¼ cup sugar

Zest of ½ lemon (optional)

1 tsp. vanilla extract

Pinch of salt

Oil, for frying

Powdered sugar

Strawberry jam (optional)

1. In a large bowl, mix together the flour, cheese, eggs, canola oil, sugar, lemon zest, vanilla extract and a pinch of salt. Leave to rest for about 30 minutes.

2. Pour oil into a small, deep pot so it comes up about 7 cm.

3. Using a spoon, make small balls with the dough. Working in batches, drop them into the hot oil and fry until golden. Transfer to a wire rack or a paper-towel lined plate.

4. Top with powdered sugar and serve with strawberry jam, if you like.

Serves 6

Tu Bishvat:
Dried Fruit and Nut Cookies

These cookies are a cross between biscotti and granola bars. They're sweet enough to feel like a treat and healthy enough to serve as a nice breakfast. Since they're packed with fruit and nuts, these cookies are perfect for Tu Bishvat (the new year for trees, often referred to as Jewish Arbor Day).

200 g (6½ oz) **chopped mixed nuts** (walnuts, hazelnuts, almonds or other)

200 g (6½ oz) **chopped mixed dried fruit** (dates, figs, raisins or other)

7 Tbs. whole wheat flour

½ tsp. baking powder

4 Tbs. brown or white sugar

2 eggs

1. Preheat the oven to 170°C/350°F.

2. Mix all the ingredients together in a large bowl.

3. Pour into a greased or parchment paper-lined loaf pan and bake for about 30 minutes, until evenly browned on top.

4. Remove from the oven and cool fully. Slice into thin slices and serve.

TIP: For crispy cookies place the thin slices in a baking pan and bake again for 5 minutes. Cool and serve.

Makes at least 40 cookies

Purim:
Hamantaschen

Yiddish for "Haman's Pockets," these filled, three-cornered cookies are eaten on the holiday of Purim, which celebrates the escape of the Jews from the evil character of Haman. This poppy seed filling is the most popular, but sometimes they have jam, dates, or even chocolate instead.

For the Dough:

3½ cups all-purpose flour

½ cup finely ground almonds

275 g (9 oz) butter

1 cup powdered sugar

3 Tbs. sugar

1 tsp. baking powder

2 eggs

Pinch of salt

For the Filling:

1½ cups milk or orange juice

1 cup sugar

3 cups ground poppy seeds

3 Tbs. honey

Lemon zest (optional)

To Serve:

Powdered sugar

1. Sift together the flour and ground almonds.

2. In a separate bowl, cream together the butter, powdered sugar and sugar until fully combined and light in color.

3. Add the sifted flour and almonds, baking powder, eggs and salt and knead until a dough is formed.

4. Press the dough into a rectangular shape, wrap in plastic wrap and refrigerate for at least 1 hour.

5. Meanwhile, make the filling. Put the milk or orange juice, sugar and poppy seeds in a pot and cook for 15 minutes, stirring occasionally. Add the honey and lemon zest, if using, and cook for another 5 minutes. Remove from the heat and allow to cool.

6. Preheat the oven to 180°C/350°F.

7. Roll out the dough to a thin, even layer and cut out circles with a cookie cutter.

8. Put about ½ teaspoon of filling in the middle of each circle. Fold up the dough into a triangle and pinch the edges. Transfer to a parchment-lined baking sheet.

9. Bake for about 10 minutes, until golden. Remove from the oven and allow to cool slightly.

10. Dust with powdered sugar and serve.

TIP: Avoid over-kneading shortbread dough like this to ensure that it crisps.

Makes at least 40

Passover:
Passover Rolls

During Passover, you cannot eat leavened bread. This clever recipe, which I learned from my grandmother, gets around that rule by using matzo meal.

2 cups water

½ cup oil

1 tsp. salt

2 cups matzo flour

4 eggs

1. Put the water, oil and salt in a deep sauté pan and bring to a boil.

2. Add the matzo flour and mix well.

3. Remove from the heat and mix in the eggs one at a time, mixing well after each addition.

4. Wet your hands and form 20 or so balls.

5. Put in a baking pan and leave to rest for 20 minutes.

6. Meanwhile, preheat the oven to 180°C/350°F.

7. Bake for 40 to 50 minutes, until lightly browned.

Variation:

• Add 1 tsp. sugar to the water along with the oil and salt to make sweet rolls.

Makes about 20

Passover Brownies

These brownies use matzo flour instead of regular flour to make them kosher for Passover. But you'd never guess it! They're rich and chocolaty, just as a brownie should be.

¾ cup matzo flour

1 cup sugar

20 g (1 Tbs.) vanilla sugar

150 g (5 oz) bittersweet chocolate

75 g (2½ oz) butter

2 eggs

¼ cup brandy

¼-½ cup roughly chopped walnuts

¼-½ cup chocolate chips (optional)

1. Preheat oven to 170°C/340°F.

2. Mix together the matzo flour, sugar and vanilla sugar. Set aside.

3. Melt the chocolate and butter together over low heat until smooth.

4. Mix the melted chocolate into the flour mixture. Add the eggs, brandy, walnuts and chocolate chips, if using, and stir to incorporate.

5. Pour into a greased 20x30-cm. baking pan and bake for about 25 minutes, until a toothpick inserted in the center comes out dry.

Serves 8 to 12

Passover:
Almond Chocolate Chip Cookies

I came up with these cookies because I wanted to offer a fun, Kosher for Passover dessert for kids. They have a great, crunchy texture and perfectly sweet flavor that makes them great all year round.

100 g (3⅓ oz) butter

½ cup sugar

1 egg

⅓ cup matzo flour
(substitute all-purpose flour)

½ cup chocolate chips

2 cups almond slivers

1. Preheat the oven to 150°C/300°F.

2. Put the butter and sugar in the bowl of a stand mixer and cream together until light and fluffy.

3. Add the egg and flour and mix to combine.

4. Gently mix in the chocolate chips and almonds.

5. Using a small cookie scoop or a tablespoon, drop 30 or so balls of dough onto 1 or 2 parchment-lined baking sheets.

6. Bake for about 15 minutes, until golden brown.

7. Transfer to wire racks and cool.

Makes about 30

Shavuot:
Cheesecake

I learned how to make this creamy, delicate cheesecake from a relative many years ago and it became a family favorite. My son loves it so much he requests it for his birthday every year. It's also perfect for Shavuot, which is celebrated with lots of cheese and dairy dishes.

For the Dough:

80 g (2 ¾ oz) butter

1 cup self-rising flour

2 Tbs. sugar

2 egg yolks (reserve whites for cake)

For the Filling:

750 g (26½ oz) soft white cheese like Israeli "ski" (substitute whipped cream cheese)

3 eggs and 2 whites

1 cup sugar

1 tsp. vanilla extract

For Topping:

2 cups lowfat sour cream

20 g (1½ Tbs.) vanilla sugar

1. Preheat the oven to 190°C/375°F.

2. Mix together the dough ingredients by hand or in a stand mixer until well combined. Press into a deep, 26-cm cake pan so it evenly covers the bottom. Bake about 10 minutes, until golden.

3. Remove from the oven, set aside and lower the oven to 170°C/340°F.

4. Mix together the white cheese, eggs and egg whites, sugar and vanilla extract. Pour over the pre-baked dough and bake for 50 minutes.

5. Mix together the sour cream and vanilla sugar and pour on top of the cake. Don't be afraid - the pan might look very full but it will deflate slightly.

6. Bake for an additional 10 minutes.

7. Remove from the oven and allow to cool to room temperature. Cover and refrigerate overnight before serving. The longer it stays in the fridge (for 1 to 2 days) the better!

Makes 1 cake

Shavuot:
Semolina Delight

This is dish that my grandmother, mother, and aunts all used to make.
It is a light and sweet treat that I make often as it contains protein
and calcium, which are especially important for children.
The dairy makes it a perfect dish for Shavuot.

2 cups milk

4 Tbs. fine semolina

3 Tbs. sugar

½ Tbs. rose water

Almonds (optional)

1. Put the milk, semolina and sugar in a pot and bring to a boil, stirring occasionally.

2. Add the rose water and keep stirring constantly over a low flame for 2 to 3 minutes, until the mixture thickens.

3. Pour into a serving platter, bowl, or rimmed baking sheet. Mark the serving portions with a knife. Decorate each portion with an almond, if you like.

4. Allow to cool, cover and allow to set in the refrigerator before serving.

Serves 8 to 10

I may be a nutritionist, but I love **Sweets** *as much as the next person. I started my 'kitchen career' at the age of 10 by baking cakes and making desserts at home. I used to make fancy cakes with layers and cream and would spend a great deal of time decorating them. Nowadays I mostly make simple but tasty desserts that focus more on flavor than appearances*

Tahini and Almond Cookies | Date and Walnut Pinwheel Cookies | Chocolate and Halva Babka | Cinnamon Rolls | Fruit Tahini Crumble | Apple Cake | Plum Cake | Cinnamon Cake | Coconut and Chocolate Cake | Orange, Semolina and Coconut Cake | Malabi

Tahini and Almond Cookies

Tahini cookies are common in Israel and I've tried a number of recipes over the years. This was the favorite of my daughters. The first time I made them with rye flour it was a mistake, but it turned out so well I've used it ever since.

1 cup all-purpose flour

1 cup rye or whole wheat flour

1 cup ground almonds (almond flour)

150 g (5 oz) cold unsalted butter, cut into cubes

¾ cup sugar

1 tsp. vanilla extract

Pinch of salt

2 Tbs. water

1 cup pure tahini

Almond slivers, optional

1. Preheat oven to 175°C/350°F. Line two baking sheets with parchment paper.

2. In a food processor, blend the flours, ground almonds, butter, sugar, vanilla and salt and process until the mixture resembles coarse crumbs.

3. Add water and tahini and process until smooth dough begins to form. Transfer to a bowl and chill for about 30 minutes to make it easier to work with.

4. Knead the dough a few times on the counter until smooth. If the dough feels very dry, dampen your hands and knead the dough slightly. If it is still too dry add a few drops of water if necessary.

5. With slightly wet hands, create small balls of the dough. Place them on the baking sheet, then flatten each one slightly with your fingers. If you like, press an almond sliver into the top of each cookie.

6. Bake for 12 to 14 minutes, or until golden brown.

7. Cool completely and serve.

Variation:

• Roll the balls of cookie dough in sugar before flattening them.

Make about 100

Date and Walnut Pinwheel Cookies

These delightful cookies are a variation on traditional Arab cookies called maamul.
While maamul cookies are stuffed, these are rolled, which is even easier.

For the Dough:

2½ cups self-rising flour

¼ cup semolina

½ cup orange juice or milk

2 eggs

200 g (6½ oz) butter, softened

¼ cup sugar

1 tsp. vanilla

¼ tsp. rose or citrus essence or
1 tsp. rose water

For the Filling:

200 gr (6½ oz) date spread

1 tsp. cinnamon powder

¼ tsp. ground cloves

¼ tsp. rose citrus essence

1 cup chopped walnuts

For Serving:

Powdered sugar

1. Preheat the oven to 170°C/340°F.

2. Mix together all the ingredients for the dough into smooth, flexible paste.

3. Press the dough into a rectangular shape, wrap in plastic wrap and let rest for at least 30 minutes in the refrigerator.

4. To prepare the filling, melt the date spread with 3 tablespoons boiling water. Add the cinnamon, cloves and rose essence and stir to combine.

5. Spread the date mixture on the flat dough and sprinkle with walnuts.

6. Roll each dough into a tight log and place in a baking pan. cut to mark the slices with a knife (see picture)

7. Bake for 35 minutes, until brown.

8. Remove from the oven and allow to cool slightly. Slice and sprinkle with powdered sugar.

TIPs: 1. See p. 200.

2. Roll dough between two floured pieces of parchment paper to prevent it from sticking.

Makes about 40 cookies

Chocolate and Halva Babka

This braided yeast cake with chocolate and halva is a favorite in the Jewish repertoire.
I add halva crumbs, a popular Middle Eastern sweet, to give it a little added texture and flavor.

Dough

560 g (18 oz) all-purpose flour

1 Tbs. dry yeast

100 g (3⅓ oz) sugar

100 g (3⅓ oz) butter, softened

2 eggs

¾ cup milk

1 tsp. salt

1 tsp. vanilla extract

Filling

Chocolate spread

Halva crumbs

Coating

1 egg, lightly beaten

1. Put all the dough ingredients in a large mixing bowl and knead by hand or in a stand mixer until a smooth and flexible dough forms. Make sure the salt doesn't touch the yeast directly.

2. Cover loosely with a dish towel and allow to rise until doubled in volume.

3. Roll out the dough on a lightly floured surface into a large rectangle about ½-inch thick.

4. Cover the dough with the chocolate spread and sprinkle generously with halva crumbs.

5. Roll up lengthwise into a tight log and press down slightly to seal. Cut the log in half.

6. Slice one of the log halves in half lengthwise down the middle and loosely twist together to form a braid. Repeat with the remaining dough log.

7. Transfer each braid to a parchment-lined loaf pan and brush with egg. Set aside and allow to rise for another 15 minutes.

8. Meanwhile, preheat the oven to 170°C/340°F.

9. Bake the babka for about 20-25 minutes until golden. Allow to cool slightly before slicing.

TIPs: 1. *Leave the dough in the refrigerator overnight to rise.*

2. *For a richer flavor, make a syrup of ¾ cup sugar, ⅔ cup water and 1 tablespoon lemon juice. Pour over the babka and serve.*

Makes 2 loaves

Cinnamon Rolls

Unlike American-style cinnamon buns, which often feature a cream cheese dough and creamy glaze, these are the variety that we enjoy most often in Israel. They have a similar yeast dough as the babka with a different filling.

For the Dough:

⅔ cup milk

1 large egg

50 g (1½ oz.) butter, softened

2 Tbs. vegetable oil or heavy cream

3½ cups flour

1 tsp. salt

1 Tbs. dry yeast

⅓ cup sugar

For the Filling and Topping:

50 g (1½ oz.) very soft butter

¾ cup brown sugar

1½ Tbs. cinnamon

1 egg, lightly beaten

For the Syrup:

½ cup sugar

¾ cup water

1. Knead all the dough ingredients together until a smooth and flexible dough forms.

2. Cover with a dish towel and allow to rise until doubled in volume.

3. Put the dough on a lightly floured surface, divide in two parts and roll out to a large rectangle about ½-inch thick.

4. Spread the soft butter over the dough. Mix together the brown sugar and cinnamon and sprinkle it over the butter. Gently roll once with a rolling pin to press down slightly.

5. Roll the dough into a tight log and press down slightly.

6. Using a sharp knife, cut into 1½-cm slices and put on a parchment paper-lined baking sheet.

7. Brush the tops with egg and let sit for 15 minutes.

8. Meanwhile, preheat the oven to 180°C/350°F.

9. Bake the cinnamon buns for about 10 minutes, until golden brown.

10. Meanwhile, put the sugar and water in a pot and heat until the sugar has dissolved.

11. Remove the cinnamon buns from the oven and brush with the hot syrup. Allow to cool slightly before serving.

Makes about 30

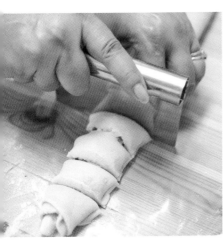

Fruit and Tahini Crumble

I really enjoy using tahini in sweets, so when I saw a similar recipe years ago I was immediately inspired. Tahini is such a common ingredient in Israel that I love to show my students different and unusual ways to use it.

4 cups chopped, mixed fruit
(use whatever is in season, such as pear, apple, strawberries, or any stone fruit or berries)

1 Tbs. lemon juice

2 Tbs. sugar

Dash of ground cinnamon

5-10 allspice berries

Whole cardamom (optional)

Star anise (optional)

¾ cup whole wheat flour

½ cup rolled oats

⅓ cup pure tahini

¾ cup light brown sugar

50 g (1½ oz.) cold butter, diced

1. Preheat the oven to 170°C/340°F.

2. Arrange the fruit in a 26-cm baking dish. Sprinkle the lemon juice, sugar and spices on top and mix.

3. In a medium bowl, mix together the flour, oats, tahini, brown sugar and butter with your fingers (or pulse in a food processor) until you obtain a crumbly texture.

4. Sprinkle the crumble evenly over the fruits.

5. Bake for 30 minutes, until the top is golden and the juices are bubbling up.

6. Remove from the oven and allow to cool slightly before serving.

7. Serve with vanilla ice cream.

Serves 8 to 10

Apple Cake

This is my family's favorite apple cake and it's very easy to make. It's a wonderful dessert or tea time snack and is especially delicious with a scoop of vanilla ice cream.

2 green apples, unpeeled and diced

3 eggs

1½ cup brown sugar

¼ cup sweet red wine

½ cup vegetable oil

1 tsp. cinnamon

Pinch of salt

1½ cups whole wheat flour

1 tsp. baking powder

Handful of raisins or walnuts
(optional)

1. Preheat the oven to 170°C/340°F.

2. Mix together all the ingredients in a large bowl by hand or in a mixer.

3. Pour the batter into a large, greased cake pan and bake for 45 to 50 minutes, until a toothpick inserted in the center comes out clean.

4. Serve warm with vanilla ice cream.

Makes 1 cake

Plum Cake

During plum season in Israel you'll always find a recipe for some variation of this famous cake in the paper. It's a wonderful way to highlight fresh plums in the summer.

For the Cake:

4 eggs

1¼ cups light brown sugar

1¾ cups self-rising flour*

100 g (3 ⅓ oz) butter

⅓ cup vegetable oil

Pinch of salt

4-6 plums, halved and pitted

For the Topping:

Cinnamon

2 Tbs. light brown sugar

1. Preheat the oven to 180°C/350°F.

2. Mix together all cake ingredients except the plums in a large bowl until the butter is fully combined (in a stand mixer or by hand).

3. Pour the batter into a large cake pan.

4. Arrange the plums on top, skin side down and sprinkle with cinnamon and brown sugar.

5. Bake for 45 to 50 minutes, until a toothpick inserted in the middle comes out dry. Remove from the oven and allow to cool slightly before cutting.

6. Serve warm with vanilla ice cream.

* If you don't have self-rising flour, add 1 teaspoon baking powder to 1¾ cup all-purpose flour.

Variation:

• Use nectarines instead of plums.

Cinnamon Cake

This is a super moist, amazingly delicious coffee cake with a lovely crumb on top. It's wonderful in the morning, with afternoon tea, or for dessert.

For the Cake:

1¾ cups plus 2 Tbs. whole wheat flour

1 heaping tsp. baking powder

2 eggs

½ cup canola oil

100 g (3⅓ oz) butter

200 ml (6½ oz) sour cream or yogurt

2 cups brown sugar

For the Topping:

1 tsp. cinnamon

¼ cup sugar

Chopped pecans

1. Preheat the oven to 170°C/340°F.

2. Mix together all the cake ingredients in a large bowl.

3. In a small bowl, mix together the cinnamon and sugar.

4. Pour half of the cake batter into a large cake pan. Sprinkle half of the cinnamon-sugar and pecans over, then top with the remaining batter. Sprinkle the remaining cinnamon-sugar and pecans over the top.

5. Bake for about 50 minutes, until a toothpick inserted in the center comes up clean.

6. Remove from the oven and allow to cool slightly before serving.

Variation:

- Use toasted pecans or walnuts.

Makes 1 cake

Coconut and Chocolate Cake

This delectable cake couldn't be easier to make and is a fun riff on the usual chocolate cake. The coconut gives it a lighter texture and taste, while the sweet red wine in the topping gives it a flavor boost.

For the Cake:

4 eggs

1 cup sugar

1 cup flour

10 g (1 Tbs.) baking powder

1 cup coconut flakes

100 g (3 ⅓ oz) grated dark chocolate

½ cup vegetable oil

Handful of walnuts (optional)

For the Topping:

½ cup sweet red wine

¼ cup water

¼ cup sugar

1. Preheat the oven to 170°C/340°F.

2. Mix all the cake ingredients together in a large bowl.

3. Pour batter into a large cake pan and bake 45 to 50 minutes, until a toothpick inserted in the center comes out dry.

4. Heat the wine, water and sugar in a small pot until sugar dissolves. Pour over the cake and serve warm with vanilla ice cream (if serving the cake warm serve with cool syrup and if the cake is cold serve it with warm syrup).

Makes 1 cake

Orange, Semolina and Coconut Cake

This is my version of a traditional Egyptian-style cake called "basbousa," which means "just a kiss." You can find variations on semolina cake across many cultures and I chose to include this one because oranges are identified so strongly with Israeli flavors. This is very nice served with sliced fresh strawberries.

For the cake:

4 eggs, whites and yolks separated

¾ cup sugar

1 cup shredded coconut

1 cup flour

10 g (1 Tbs.) baking powder

10 g (1 Tbs.) vanilla sugar

1 cup fine semolina

1 cup orange juice

¾ cup canola oil

Zest of 1 orange

For the Syrup:

¾ cup sugar

1 cup water

Juice of ½ lemon

1. Preheat the oven to 170°C/340°F.

2. Beat the egg whites with the sugar until soft peaks form.

3. Mix together the shredded coconut, flour, baking powder, vanilla sugar and semolina.

4. In a separate bowl, mix together the egg yolks, orange juice, canola oil and orange zest.

5. Add the egg yolk mixture to the dry ingredients and mix to combine.

6. Gently fold the egg whites into the batter.

7. Pour into a greased 26-cm cake pan and bake for 30 to 40 minutes, until a toothpick inserted in the center comes up clean.

8. Meanwhile, prepare the syrup: Put the sugar, water and lemon juice in a small pot and heat until the sugar dissolves. Cool.

9. When the cake is out of the oven, pour the cooled syrup over the top and wait 10 minutes before serving.

TIP: *When the cake is hot, serve with cold syrup and when the cake is cold serve with hot syrup.*

Makes 1 cake

Malabi

This luscious milk pudding is popular throughout the Middle East and is beloved in Israel.
The texture is light and creamy and the rosewater gives the dessert a beautiful,
delicate flavor.

2 cups milk or coconut milk

5 Tbs. corn starch

½ Tbs. rose water

½ cup cream

¼ cup sugar

For serving:

Chopped almonds, pistachios and/
or strawberry syrup

1. Put ½ cup of the milk in a bowl with the corn starch and rose water and mix until you have a smooth, even mixture.

2. Put the cream, sugar and remaining 1½ cups milk in a pot and bring to a boil. Lower the heat, add the corn starch mixture and cook for 2 to 3 minutes, stirring constantly, until the mixture thickens

3. Pour into serving bowls and cool to room temperature. Transfer to the fridge to chill for 4 hours, or overnight.

4. Drizzle with strawberry syrup and sprinkle with nuts just before serving.

TIP: To make the recipe parve and vegan,
replace the milk with coconut milk.

Serves 6 to 8

Acknowledgments

"Showing gratitude is one of the simplest yet most powerful things humans can do for each other."

Randy Pausch, The Last Lecture

Honestly my cooking turned into a cookbook thanks to my family, friends and professional team, each of whom contributed so much.

I am so very grateful to my family, especially my dearest husband Ben who is always with me. He's the best sous-chef a cook could ask for and is an indispensible help during my cooking classes and throughout the making of this book. I am also very thankful to my children Dan, Dorine and Daniella, who encourage and support me and showed lots of patience during the cooking and shooting period for the book.

I am so very grateful to my dearest mom who built my cooking and baking confidence by opening her kitchen to me since I was very young. Her pantry was always full, which permitted me to find ingredients and make something spontaneously. So is the pantry in my home today.

I thank all my guests who came to cook with me and enjoyed the food and the experience. I would especially like to thank Chef Zov from California who encouraged me to write this book by telling me so simply to "just do it," so I did.

My genuine appreciation and thanks to Katherine Martinelli and Idit Yatzkan, who worked with me like we were an old team with such ease and harmony. Katherine is a talented food photographer and writer with so much passion. She took the photos you see in the book in my home with no special conditions. She tasted all the food and watched the preparations and did a terrific job editing.

Idit is a professional designer who made me think about so many different aspects about the book, I really learned a lot. Her way of designing the book was emphasizing the photos. She made it look simply amazing and tangible. Thank you again with all my heart Katherine and Idit.

Last thank you to all my friends who came to taste the dishes and approved them for the book.
Orly

Index

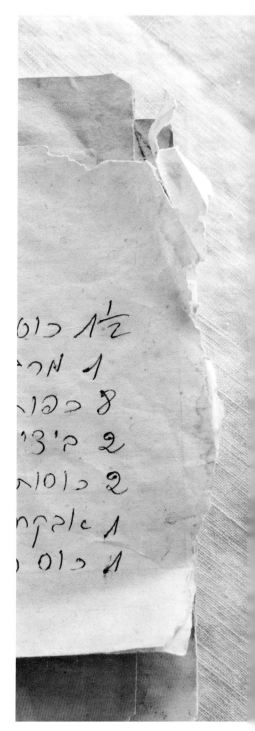

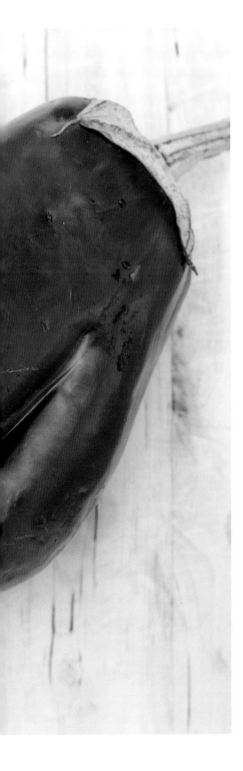